Fighting Mad

Practical Solutions
for
Conquering Anger

DR. RAY GUARENDI

servant
AN IMPRINT OF
FRANCISCAN MEDIA
Cincinnati, Ohio

Cover design by Candle Light Studios
Book design by Mark Sullivan

LIBRARY OF CONGRESS CATALOGING-IN-PUBLICATION DATA
Guarendi, Raymond.
Fighting mad : practical solutions for conquering anger / Dr. Ray Guarendi.
pages cm
Includes bibliographical references and index.
ISBN 978-1-61636-707-7 (alk. paper)
1. Anger. I. Title.
BF575.A5G83 2013
152.4'7—dc23
2013037603

Published by Servant, an imprint of
Franciscan Media
28 W. Liberty St.
Cincinnati, OH 45202
www.FranciscanMedia.org

Printed in the United States of America.
Printed on acid-free paper.
16 17 18 19 20   5 4 3 2

· · · · · · ·

To my brother, Mike,
my best buddy growing up.
My best friend now.

· · · · · · ·

Acknowledgments

· · · · · · ·

Thank you....

To Claudia Volkman, my editor at Servant, who makes it all easier to move through the book-publishing world with her gentle, competent guidance.

To Cindy Cavnar, a former editor who asked me, "Did you ever think about writing a book about anger?" Hopefully her request was based upon my clinical experience and not a personality flaw.

To Misty Woodrum and Molly Romano, who typed and re-typed, learning a second language in the process: my hand-written, semi-legible, re-edited scrawl.

Contents

. . . .

Chapter One

. . . .

ANGER or ISSUES?

. . . .

"He has a short fuse."

"She's so emotional."

"He's got a temper."

Once upon a time these were everyday assessments of someone lacking in self-control or getting upset too easily. The descriptions were straightforward—some might say, too broad—and most people knew what they meant. They came from a common language, spoken by both the educated and the not so. They provided the base from which to begin figuring out exactly what was the issue—oops, I mean *trouble*.

In today's ongoing and on-growing preoccupation with all things psychological, shirt-sleeve expressions are often dismissed as too simplistic, failing to fully nuance the dynamics. More therapeutic language is in vogue: "He has a low frustration tolerance." "She displays deficits in emotional regulation." "He struggles with anger management issues." This last one is the reigning diagnosis for anyone who gets upset too easily.

By linguistic osmosis, parents too have picked up a contemporary emotion speak. Fewer talk of tantrums or bad attitudes. Instead the assessments are more clinical: "He's an angry child." "She has problems with impulse control." "His moods look bipolar."

The new language avoids value judgments. At school little Butch's aggression isn't wrong; it's unacceptable. His actions aren't bad; they're inappropriate choices. He isn't being mean; he's exhibiting relational deficits. If he keeps this up, he could lose not one but two stickers from his reward chart.

Fancy language does sound smart. It conveys the impression that one understands what really is going on below the surface. What good is my PhD if I can't use multisyllabic words?

Shortly after my graduation from college, my father asked me about an acquaintance who was acting bizarre, out of touch with reality. I offered my years-of-training assessment: "It sounds as if her thinking is getting crazy."

My dad chided me, "Ray, you're a professional. Is that how you talk?" Maybe Pop was beginning to have second thoughts about paying for all that schooling.

Had I known the person more closely, maybe I could have talked more professionally. Still, I offered a basic and, as it turned out, accurate first impression.

My father didn't finish high school the first time around. He received his GED at age fifty-nine, the oldest kid in his class. Like many of his generation, Pop had a way of cutting to the heart of a matter with few words. Once I asked him why one of his friends was so unreliable, wanting psychological nuance and family analysis. Pop answered, "He's always been just a big talker." To the point, on target. How come he was allowed to be so succinct, and I couldn't say "crazy thinking"?

For all its bookishness, the new language can be as fuzzy as the old language. What exactly does "symptoms of emotional dysregulation" mean? Or what about "social dysfunction manifesting itself in interpersonal deficits"? A small circle of experts may have some agreement about their definition, but who else? "He has a temper" may also need some specifics attached to it, but at least it doesn't evoke a "Huh?"

A parallel can be noted in medicine. Many medical labels diagnose a condition or illness: type I diabetes, amyotrophic lateral sclerosis, macular degeneration. Know the name; know its causes and treatments.

Other labels are learned-sounding names for some everyday stuff: hidrosis, ascites, syncope—or sweating, swelling, and fainting. These describe physical symptoms; they don't diagnose underlying causes or treatments.

"Deficits in impulse regulatory mechanisms" carries more biological oomph than "short fuse." Nonetheless, both speak to the same trouble: emotions or behavior poorly controlled. The former just speaks in a more erudite voice.

All of this is not to say that we should jettison every piece of modern anger talk. Language evolves whether we want it to or not. Nor is it a call to oversimplify the many shades and shapes of anger. My working domain as a psychologist includes the language and complexities of anger. But the message is: Much talk about anger these days needn't be so academic. You don't have to sound smart about something to be smart about something.

Science has a principle called the law of parsimony. Ironically, *parsimony* is an obtuse word to describe this principle. Put simply it means, "Seek the simplest explanation." A complex answer is not needed, nor necessarily correct, when a more straightforward one will do. Becoming too complex too fast carries the risk of directing one away from a clear understanding. The law of parsimony applies well to human behavior.

Parents ask me, "Why does my three-year-old melt down when he doesn't get his way?" (Admit it, "melt down" does paint the picture well.) Often I reply, "Because he's three." I do get paid for such depth. While we then look more closely at their discipline and family life, at a most fundamental level, "Because he's three" does answer the question.

Am I wrestling with words? "Temper" or "emotional regulatory issues": Don't they point to the same reality? Yes and no.

Yes in that, whatever it's called, anger let loose too easily and too often has bad social repercussions. The person on the receiving end of another's anger isn't going to feel mollified knowing he was the target not of a temper but of an emotional dysfunction.

No in that, as the psychoanalyzing terms multiply, the sense of personal responsibility divides. If I am beset by a so-called anger management condition, is some vague malfunction of my psyche at the root of my agitation? I'm not the one who's acting wrongly; it's my affliction that's moving me. And the more wrongly I act, the more evidence for my affliction.

The reasoning travels in circles. Why is he so easily upset? Because he has anger management issues. How do you know he has anger management issues? Because he's so easily upset.

To better understand anger and its emotional buddies, this book will avoid ever-shifting newspeak. It will start with a core truth: Whatever it's called, for most of us most of the time, anger and its causes lie well within our control.

I am the one who engages the emotion, and I am the one who can stoke or stop its ugly expression. I possess the intellect and will to "regulate my impulses."

TURNING THE PAGE...

Anything that is innate to the human condition will spur new terms in the effort to comprehend it. The risk lies in the tendency to let new terms cloud rather than clear understanding.

Anger can nestle around your personal edges or rest smack in the middle of your being. How much it bothers you or others often depends upon whether you or they see it as a problem or a disorder.

Chapter Two

· · · · · · ·

PROBLEM or DISORDER?

· · · · · · ·

A mother worries that her very active six-year-old son is hyperactive. A teacher questions whether a defiant student has a conduct disorder. A wife wonders whether her husband's pull to all things Internet is an addiction.

Much of how we analyze ourselves and others these days falls under the shadow of "Is there a more serious condition here, maybe a psychological disorder?" Are we looking at standard human stuff, or is this picture out of the norm? And how far out of the norm is too far?

This mindset lies beneath many of the questions I'm asked:

"My seven-year-old hit me twice last week during a tantrum. Is that typical for his age?"

"My husband comes home from work irritated almost every night. Do most men do that?"

"I just seem to get upset over the littlest things. Am I losing it?"

My answer to this last one: Losing what? Your composure? Probably. Your mental balance? Probably not.

"Is it normal?" is a question propelled by a rising tsunami of diagnoses, some accepted by clinicians, others coined in pop psychology. Ironically, some of the most well-known of conditions are not even professionally recognized diagnoses. Think middle child syndrome or midlife crisis.

The template is stock: Identify a problem in living; observe a cluster of related complications; attach a label; create a syndrome. Some of these newfound disorders come with signs that, to some degree, can envelop many if not most people.

Who hasn't come across a magazine article, heard some expert, or read on the Internet about a recently discovered affliction and thought, "That sounds a lot like me"? Or the more universal, "That sounds a lot like my (fill in the blank) husband, mother, friend, boss, son, second cousin once removed, dog."

There are any number of professional diagnoses that list anger as a symptom. Some call it a primary symptom: intermittent explosive disorder, impulse control disorder, oppositional defiant disorder. Others call it a secondary one: adult antisocial disorder, conduct disorder, borderline personality disorder.

Much of the time someone close—a spouse, parent, friend, or teacher—is the first to question the severity of the trouble. "Do you think there's a deeper issue here? Have you thought about getting professional help?"

How deep does an issue have to descend in order to be a disorder? And when does it call for outside help? Can I fix it myself, or do I need a trained hand?

How does a trained hand decide? How does she judge whether to advise counseling? The key word here is *judge*. The borders of many diagnoses are not clear-cut; they require interpretation. Much diagnosis comes down to opinion. Do a person's actions or feelings fall within the outlines of a label?

Consider oppositional-defiant disorder (ODD, as it is popularly known), arguably the most prevalent childhood diagnosis. Basically it describes an unruly and difficult youngster, hence oppositional and defiant. What makes him so? For some it's inborn temperament: They're wired more fiery. For most it's due to family or parenting—instability, little or no discipline, emotionally harsh conditions.

ODD is a summary label for what was once thought to be a lot of bad or wrong behavior. Is the child aggressive? Does he show anger? Often the assumption is drawn that there is some internal dysfunction at work. But in actuality the label is attached because someone has judged the behavior too ugly and too uncontrolled too often. In short, ODD is not the cause of the conduct; it's a name for it.

Consider the adult diagnosis intermittent explosive disorder. Its cardinal feature is "severe discrete episodes of failure to resist aggressive impulses." What defines *severe*? Is an eruption during a heated basketball game as foul as one aimed at one's mother, assuming she wasn't the player who shoved you into the ref? How many discrete episodes total a disorder? Over what period of time: a month, a year, a decade, since joining the basketball league?

How intense must the aggressive impulses be to constitute a failure to resist? What if I feel a near overwhelming urge to kick the ref but instead curse? What if instead of screaming a stream of epithets that can be heard outside the gym, I yell one shocking sentence? Am I failing to resist my impulses, or am I moderating them?

In medicine, diabetes is determined by a number—blood sugar level. So are other conditions—hypothyroidism (thyroid hormone level), anemia (blood iron level), heart failure (ejection fraction). What are the numbers above or below which a problem with anger becomes a disorder? Decibel level? Curse words per hour? Tools thrown? Repetitions of "I've had enough"?

Marking a clear boundary between normal and abnormal, between problem and disorder, is frustrated by the inexactness of language. As the shrinks would admit, anger is hard to operationally define.

Further, a preoccupation with the term *normal* narrows the boundaries of what is defined as normal, leading more behaviors to be seen as potentially deviant. Parents in increasing numbers, for example, ask me if I think their adolescents' emotional surges are normal. I always thought *adolescent* and *emotional* were pretty much synonymous.

"Is it normal?" is pushing aside far more relevant questions, like "Is it right?" or "What should I do about it?" If I'm acting or reacting worse than most would, do I first need to uncover just how unusual I might be? If thirty-three of a hundred people would behave just as I in similar circumstances, am I out of line but not wildly so? How about if only seventeen would? Six?

Conversely, if I'm normal—as I see it, anyway—does this mean I don't need to change or that my behavior is not hurting others? "I'm normal" can serve as a justification for not looking at oneself. Something can be quite common and still cause lots of trouble. Think sin.

Suppose, however, that eighty-two out of a hundred psychologists agree that my outbursts fit with intermittent explosive disorder. What's the next step? What should be the treatment?

In most cases some form of talk therapy is recommended—individual, couples, group, an anger management course. All can help, and the diagnosis itself doesn't tell me which one will. Good intervention focuses on what's going on with the person rather than the name of what's going on.

The one-tantrum-per-day child as well as the one-tantrum-per-hour child would likely benefit from a firmer parental hand, so to speak. While Brutus may learn self-control more quickly than his feistier sibling, Harmony, toning down both kids essentially involves the same measures. One child just takes longer to teach than the other.

Disordered or not? The question is often unnecessary, even irrelevant. Benefit comes from being open to change. Sometimes that change is aided by a counselor, sometimes by a clergy, sometimes by a spouse, sometimes by a friend, sometimes by a book. Always it involves oneself.

An individual who erupts in a major way over minor frustrations may or may not need or seek counseling. What he does need is to personally decide to better control his "discrete episodes of failure to resist aggressive impulses."

TURNING THE PAGE...

Whatever a problem is called, the first word in self-improvement is *self*. It is the resolve to face and face down one's uglier impulses. It is, if you will, the will to will. And how much will is needed is related to whether one is wired cool or hot.

Chapter Three

. . . .

COOL or HOT?

. . . .

Aunt Esther passed away at age ninety-three. On the day she died, I was privileged to be sitting beside her bed at the nursing home. Oxygen-assisted and nearly comatose, she awoke for a few seconds, smiled at me, and proclaimed, "I like chicken. But I don't like the inside parts, just the outside, the legs and thighs."

Not realizing it at the time, I had heard her last words. She left this world some twenty minutes after I left her room. The psychologist in me couldn't resist pondering if some deeper meaning lay in her closing proclamation. Maybe a final gratitude for the simple, good things in life. Perhaps anticipation of another-world banquet. Whatever the cause, she died in a calm that reflected how she lived.

From my boyhood I seldom saw Aunt Esther show ire. To call my aunt a gentle soul would be tantamount to calling Mother Teresa a nice person. It would be an abuse of understatement.

Once, while at home alone, Aunt Esther confronted a young man who had entered her kitchen and was grabbing her purse from the table. Rising up to her full four feet ten inches, in her most intimidating voice (maybe reaching fifty decibels—roughly the sound of a purse being dropped), she commanded, "Hey, stop that, you dirty dog!" (She did every once in a while slip into vile potty mouth.) He did and left.

Was my aunt a poster child for emotional equilibrium? Or did she develop a placid demeanor as she aged? After all, one can practice a lot of self-restraint in nearly a century of life. She was a deeply religious woman. Did some of her softer spirit evolve with her faith?

I think the answers are yes, yes, and yes. A complete explanation, though, needs more. Something in my aunt's temperament, her inborn personality, underlay her equanimity. And as my mother confirmed, it was there from her beginning.

The stereotype of the sweet little old lady is grounded in reality. Lots of sweet little old ladies are out there. Many didn't need to grow old to grow sweet. At one time they were sweet little young ladies. In fact, their dispositions were pleasant when they were in diapers. Anger in whatever form was never a durable part of who they were and are.

When I attended college long ago—Freud was a freshman when I was a senior—the emphasis was on all the ways the environment shaped personality. People weren't blank slates from birth, but most of the writing on them came from outside. Actions, habits, inclinations—these were seen to be mostly shaped by one's learning. Physiology was a contributor but a lesser one. In the nature-versus-nurture competition, nurture scored the most points.

As I moved further into the world of therapy, I concluded that nature hadn't been given its due. Often I noticed links between someone's present behavior and her early tendencies. For example, an adult experiencing anxiety marked by panic attacks would routinely recall being uneasy as a young child in social situations. Or a husband whose trip-switch temper was causing marital discord would tell how from toddlerhood he took his place as the most rebellious of his parents' children.

As I moved into fatherhood, I saw up close and personal the power of temperament. Having ten children, I lived daily within a wild scattergram of personalities. One child was quiet pretty much from the womb. When asked, for instance, what he did his first day of kindergarten, in a moment of explosive self-revelation he answered, "Stuff."

Another child would detail her day in two to four hundred words per minute, with gusts up to eight hundred. Another could get irate if a sibling sneezed in the house, while one was so sanguine that he didn't realize he had siblings for his first six years. It's not all in the genes, but enough of it is.

For most people public speaking, if not at the top of the anxiety pyramid, is near the top. Just the thought of talking in front of a group can cause them social shivers. For nearly thirty years I've been a public speaker. I can't remember ever being nervous about it. Is it because I'm such a paragon of social composure? As my wife would attest, no. However it happened, I am not predisposed to that type of anxiety. It's just not part of me. Now, controlling my temperature while playing basketball, that's a different piece of wiring

Mountains of research now confirm what we nonresearchers know intuitively. All people are born with biological predispositions that move them in one direction or another in their contacts with others and in life.

To be sure, emotions are far too variable and situation responsive to be directed by one gene, or a bunch for that matter. There is no x gene that causes y behavior, certain medical conditions excepted. No single gene underlies temper, or impulsiveness, or irritability. It's an intricate dance among many genes and circumstances. There's a universal characteristic called free will that makes the picture even more unpredictable.

Therefore, one's genetics do not offer a biochemical excuse, as in, "My body made me do it." No husband will win affection from his wife by hiding behind, "Honey, I've had a temper long before I met you. You'd better learn to live with it, because it's just a part of me, and I can't change it now."

No parent of a volcanic Serena would—I hope—in resignation surrender, "She's so strong-willed. There's not much I can do but accept it. It's going to be a long fifteen years."

No, what he would accept—I hope—is that he needs five times the perseverance to teach Serena some self-control as he needs for her even-tempered brother. Success may come slowly, but for Serena's sake, as well as that of everyone near ground zero, it must be pursued.

Grown-up Serenas tell me of a lifelong battle to douse their fiery emotions. Genuinely distressed by their proclivity to overreact, their efforts are exhausting, with a two-steps-forward, one-step-back element. Still, they show an admirable will to keep advancing. They mean to conquer, or at least quiet, some of their inborn inclinations.

Science is a long way from knowing (if it ever will) how much a lack of self-control is nature and how much is nurture. And in the end it doesn't matter all that much. We have to alter for the better what we can. If not our temperament, then our temper. If not our bodies, then our minds.

Few people are Aunt Esthers, and maybe not too many would want to be. But few people are grinches either. Most of us live somewhere in the middle ground of the emotional range. And that is where the contest to moderate any unruly emotions takes place.

The good news, as we shall see, is that we possess the mental resources to overcome even our body's strongest inclinations.

TURNING THE PAGE...

Genetics, temperament, nature—all point to the same reality: Everyone is wired in ways that help or hinder the way he truly wants to live. Some of us have a higher emotional idle. And that can show in whether we simmer or boil.

Chapter Four

. . . .

SIMMER or BOIL?

. . . . . .

Ask a hundred people, "What is anger?" and most will describe the eruptive kind—the kind that surges, spikes, and slowly subsides. The more intense, the more impactful. It can be a memorable contrast to the otherwise quiet backdrop of a relationship.

If I direct ninety decibels of hurtful words toward you, not only my substance but also my style would be real hard to ignore. My emotional quake might register a six or higher on your personal Richter scale, rattling your mind with multiple afterthoughts.

If I say little or nothing, instead sustaining a sour glare, you may still sense my meaning, but it won't touch you so palpably. There remains room for you to wonder exactly what's inside me.

Eruptive anger is uglier, but to most people simmering anger is more worrisome. Eruptive anger is a visible assault. It is there for anyone to see. It doesn't take a psychologist to analyze its component parts. Anger that smolders is less detectable, more insidious. It holds the potential to silently mutate into something more blatant and shocking, something seemingly contrary to one's overall persona.

Simmering anger has a cousin; call it silent anger. In the main it's more benign and more common than the simmering variety. It lacks the seething component that feeds a desire for retribution. Silent anger is a low-level irritability or recurrent prickliness. Over time it can come to characterize, for example, one or both partners in a poor marriage. It also bedevils parents perturbed over a child's daily misbehavior.

What sustains silent anger? Not so much everyday frustrations but the meaning given to those frustrations. A parent may think, "This child is deliberately acting bad to make my life miserable." A spouse may think, "I don't mean as much to him as his work friends do." There are ways to look at others and events that fuel agitation and ways that settle it. Unfortunately, it's all too easy to think the worst first. Thinking more accurately takes practice.

If you find yourself in a stew, don't ask, "What are others doing to me to cause this?" Ask, What am I doing to me? This is a question we will unpack in greater detail in upcoming chapters.

Emotional outbursts, even when frequent, don't always point to an angry underside. They may instead point to identifiable emotional triggers. Someone who lives with an angry spouse or child knows firsthand what words or circumstances will rocket the person from settled to smoking.

A parent will ask me, "Why is my child so easily upset?"

"What do you mean?"

"Well, she gets fired up so fast, something must be underneath it all." The parent concludes that her child must be living in a state of low boil.

In fact, the child's emotional temperature most of the time is 98.6 degrees. She only steams when she is thwarted. Deny her something and her anger appears, not because it was lurking, primed to surge, but because it has become her predictable reaction to not getting her way. When the parent practices better discipline, the hidden anger usually fades, not only from sight but also from the child's being.

Can simmering and boiling anger live side by side? Can they feed one another? Sure. More often than not, though, the relationship flows in one direction. Simmering is the forerunner of boiling.

The most inexperienced cook knows that bringing a simmering pot to boil takes less heat than starting with one filled with cool water. Hot displays are indeed more likely to come from someone who simmers perpetually over wrongs. While eruptive anger can dissipate into stewing, for most people it doesn't lead to a long-term trait of stewing. Eventually the person stops dwelling on the injustice or offense. Only if he refuses to let the anger go does it become a link in a chain of internal strife.

Extreme simmering anger gets wide press when television turns its eyes upon the quiet family man who one day thoroughly shatters his emotional restraints and torches four neighbors' garages. Each neighbor in turn offers the camera a similar portrait: "He seemed like such a nice guy—always waved to me when he saw me mowing my lawn. At our last family barbeque, he even sent over a dozen ears of corn. I guess you can never really know, huh?"

Not exactly true. Genuinely calm, even-tempered individuals don't up and burn down buildings. Those who seem to inexplicably explode have, perhaps over time, cultivated a mound of resentments that finally detonated with a seemingly trivial trigger.

Signs of coming combustion often were present but were too scattered to arouse notice.

Routinely I am asked to assess the origins of someone's violence or aggression. Every so often the behavior comes from a youngster who "never gets into trouble at school" or from an adult who is "a well-liked Little League coach." What initially seems puzzling almost always becomes less so as I delve into the person's thinking, perceptions, or unspoken resentments. Upon closer look, the inexplicable becomes explicable.

The garage-assaulting family man or the punch-an-umpire popular coach appeal to social voyeurism, but even as the media play amateur analysts, such personalities are more a caricature than reality. In psychology, for the most part, what you see is what you get. Anger, quiet or loud, is usually pretty obvious.

You can be tempted to think otherwise. Suppose while bantering easily with someone, he abruptly overreacts to a comment you made. "Where did that come from? Why did he get so irate over a simple remark?" Did you unwittingly tap into a hidden reservoir of hostility? Did your words trigger some deep-seated psychological conflict?

Probably not. The explanation is more straightforward. You stumbled into a sensitive personal place. You stepped on a nerve, one you didn't know was there. Even the rawest nerves, however, aren't typically signs of emotionally percolating personalities.

Not uncommonly, one raw nerve lies below most of someone's anger. It becomes the template by which another's comments and conduct are interpreted. For example, a wife may feel undervalued by her husband. To her mind he gives her regular indications of this. She thus becomes more inclined to hear a lack of appreciation, even when none is meant.

"Mark's wife is one heck of a cook." Wife-thought, "And of course I'm not."

"Steve just told me his mother-in-law is getting easier to get along with." Wife-thought, "My mother isn't the witch you think."

Once a thought template is in place, even neutral remarks can spark reactions. Silent anger can simply be an attitude that predisposes one to look for offense.

Anger is two-faced. It can be slow-moving or rampaging. It can be wordless or wordy. It can nudge ever so imperceptibly, or it can hit with the force of a runaway truck. How anger shows itself determines how it is best managed. The silent and simmering, as we shall see, are conquered differently than are the loud and boiling.

TURNING THE PAGE...

Of all the emotions, anger is arguably the one most scrutinized yet most baffling. That's because it resists easy definition. To understand the nature of anger, one must ask about its who, what, when, and where. Put another way, is anger a trait or a state?

Chapter Five

. . . .

TRAIT or STATE?

. . . .

"He's an angry child." Parents of feisty kids tell me this a few sentences after, "His name is…" When I ask, "What makes you think so?" I hear some standard responses:

"He flares up over the littlest things."
"She reacts all out of proportion."
"She is just so easily frustrated."
"He carved 'I'm mad at this family' into the vinyl siding of our house—four times."

All right, I've yet to hear this last one. Still, the portrayals present the perception: "My child is an angry person."

"When does this anger most show itself?" I ask.

"When he's denied something or when he's disciplined."

"Is he angry at times other than those?"

"No, if we let him do whatever he wants, he's in a decent mood."

"So it's safe to say that this angry child's anger is limited to specific times and places?"

"It seems so."

"What does his teacher say?"

"I don't understand it. His teacher doesn't see any of this."

"Has he ever shown his angry self at school?"

"Never. She says he's a delight."

"How do you explain the fact that his teacher, who has a fraction of your authority, gets him to behave every day all day without so much as a whiff of defiance?"

"Do you suppose he holds it in all day, and when he gets home he has to explode?"

"Probably not. I think he knows where the speed limit is twenty and where it's the interstate."

The wife of a grouch meets a woman who regales her with "Your husband is such a joy to work with. He's so pleasant and positive with everyone. Please don't take offense at this, but a lot of the ladies there envy you."

At which wife thinks, "Yeah, well, I envy them." She has to choke back, "What's this guy's last name, and does he look like my wallet picture here?" Not only is she stung at hearing where she sits on her husband's "Be nice to" list, but she can't reconcile the image of the man she knows with that of the one those women know.

How does one reconcile the inconsistencies between home child and school child or between marital partner and work partner? Well, they don't need to be reconciled. We're talking about human beings here. The child is not one person with his parents and another with his teacher—though on the surface it may seem so. Neither is the husband one man at work and another at home. He is the same person responding to distinct environments. Different places promote different conduct.

Different places also mean different people. Aren't there those in your life who evoke very disparate sides of you? Your favorite brother-in-law is likeable and easy to be around. (I hope his wife thinks so too.) He naturally makes others feel accepted, and you're at ease around him. "Edgy" would be the last word he'd use to describe you. "Relaxed" would be his term.

Another brother-in-law can be opinionated and contrary, not just with you but also with others. Around him you are edgy and don't hide it very well. Thus he sees you as the one not easy to be around. You're just an irate person, he's concluded.

Both brothers-in-law would be surprised to hear what the other thinks. "That's not at all the person I know." In fact, both adjectives—relaxed and irate—fit you. It depends in part upon whom you're with and who is doing the describing.

As an aside, most people don't want to think they might play a role in someone's poor behavior. It's more protective of one's ego to see another's conduct as being due to his personality. "He's that way" is much more comforting than "He's that way around me."

Although doctors don't diagnose this phenomenon, parents and spouses do: It's the Dr. Jekyll–Mr. Hyde syndrome.

"My child has a Jekyll-Hyde personality. She can be totally cooperative one minute, raging the next. It's like she's two completely different kids."

"My husband is pretty pleasant with everyone except his mother. Around her he gets surly and withdrawn. It's almost as though he has a split personality."

With some rare psychiatric exceptions, there is no such thing as a split personality. It's merely a popular phrase to capture what looks like too much confusing variety in one personality. All of us have some Jekyll-Hyde in us. That is not a sign of pathology but a normal abnormality.

A child who is painfully shy in class may be rudely disrespectful with Mom or Grandma. A take-charge, abrasive woman at the office may be a quiet lady at her church. A dour father at home may be Mr. Golf Goodtime on the links. At work the boss orders others around; at home his five-year-old daughter orders him around.

We expect others to act like who they are or who we believe they are, across people, times, and places. To some degree they do. People with high moral character act morally under most conditions. Indeed, morals that come and go with the setting are really no morals at all. Every one of us, however, is a creature not only of habit but also of contrast. The circumstances (state) we're in can shape our conduct as much or more than the characteristics (traits) that describe us.

As we said two chapters ago, some people are more hot-wired biologically than the norm. Wouldn't that render them naturally angrier, or at least more easily angered, than most? Wouldn't that mean they have an anger trait? Yes and no. (As a trained communicator, I speak in definites, sort of.)

Yes, some individuals' emotional barometers are set higher than average. So they are called emotional (an overly broad label). What that really means is that they react strongly across a range of situations. String enough overreactions together, and the personality trait is attached, by themselves or by others.

But no, emotional people are not bound always and everywhere to act emotionally. They are not automatons by their wiring.

Disposition is not destiny. Even they show different temperatures with different people and in different places.

Time or, more exactly, the forces of life can reshape a personality too. A frustrated wife says, "I never saw this side of him when we were dating. Not even early in our marriage. He used to be so much easier to get along with. Is this who he really is, and I just didn't see it?"

That's not always clear. But what is clear is that personality changes can reflect relationship changes. One or both spouses now bring out the worst in the other. Said another way, the difficult partner may not be who he is but who he is in a difficult marriage.

Are these distinctions without effect? What does it matter if I'm an angry person or a person who gets angry with certain someones or somethings? Anger is still anger. Yet it does matter for a number of reasons.

One, such distinctions can reassure. Because personality defines who someone is, it is seen as something stable, resisting change or correction. Consequently, being an angry person sounds more serious than being a person who gets angry sometimes. Correcting any life problem begins with describing it correctly. Describing anger as more deep-rooted than it really is makes rectifying it seem more challenging.

Two, distinctions narrow the focus. When counseling a so-called angry child or adult, I must begin with questions—plenty. I need specifics—the who, what, when, and where of the anger's appearance. Just knowing someone is an angry person does me or him little good. The characterization is too wide to be useful. Unless I narrow it, I don't know where to head next.

Three, distinctions present solutions. Suppose I know that my abrasive Uncle Buck brings out my own abrasiveness. I can (a) keep a room or two between us at any family gathering, (b) resolve to let his opinions float past my ears into space or into someone else's ears, (c) keep my wife nearby, to push me away or pinch me if I'm tempted to retort, (d) play Legos in the basement with the preschoolers until the Buckster falls asleep or goes home.

If disciplining my kids makes me agitated for two hours afterward, what's my strategy? Should I do less talking and more action? Lots of words can lead to lots of volume can lead to lots of agitation.

Do I need to discipline sooner? If a behavior is wrong, then it's wrong whether I'm upset about it or not. It is far better to act from principle than from rushing emotions. "I'm an angry parent" may not be true. It could be better said, "I get angry when I take too long to discipline."

Whether it's with my kids or with Uncle Buck, to best fix me I need to aim where the fix is most needed. What may seem a deficit in personal self-control may be my allowing circumstances to push me too hard. I may not have an anger trait so much as a few too many anger states.

TURNING THE PAGE...

Some anger is trait anger: Something within one's nature makes one grumpier than the average bear. Other anger is better called state anger, a more or less negative reaction depending upon the setting. Knowing what sets me on edge is a first step toward smoothing my edges.

Another step is looking at the person with whom I clash. Is it someone with whom I am close?

Chapter Six

. . . .

CLOSE or CLASH?

. . . .

It's the law of emotional proximity: Those closest to us can rile us most. Spouses, parents, children, friends—those inhabiting our inner emotional circle—can draw forth our ire, sometimes with maddening repetition. Why so? These are people we love. Doesn't love lift tolerance for someone's conduct? It does, but several opposing laws operate too.

First is the law of contact. The more intimate the relationship, the more openings for misunderstanding or friction. The mail carrier and I trade a few sentences a week, if that. Our meetings remain superficially pleasant, prompting me to judge him a "pretty nice guy." My family and I connect in ways far beyond a mailbox.

The saying is cynical: Familiarity breeds contempt. Yet a distasteful kernel of truth lingers in it. The more I live around someone, the more I experience who he or she is, warts and all. And it's those warts that can chafe me. Though I must always remember, I too have my warts.

It's not much of a challenge for me to think well of all the people in India. As far as I'm aware, none of them have ever mistreated or criticized me. My family members? That's a whole different population. Not only do they reside zero to fifty feet from me, but we interact regularly. The more communication, the more chances for miscommunication. It's somewhat of a numbers game.

Of all the words I exchange with another, though the majority might promote good feelings, some can spark ill ones. Sad but true. I'm more likely to sin against those I live with, as they can emotionally most move me, up or down.

Second, the law of personalization. Emotional closeness can lead to personalizing, or reading another's actions as a comment about me or about our relationship. And my reaction to that reading can be quick and hot.

An example of personalizing: "If he acted as a husband is supposed to, he would be more considerate and decent toward me." The implication is that he doesn't care about you, or is thoughtless, or worse, is deliberately trying to antagonize you. None of which may be true in any given situation.

People have limitless reasons for acting as they do. Getting personal may or may not be in the mix. Nonetheless, the belief that another's conduct is directed right at me provokes a strong feeling, which can provoke a strong reaction. More about this in chapter 20.

A third law: the law of expectations. We expect good behavior from those close to us. The unspoken nature of relationships dictates this. As we shall see in chapter 14, the higher the expectations, the larger the gap between the way I want to be treated and the way I am treated. Hence more room for frustration.

The fourth law: the law of reciprocity. If I treat someone well, I believe she should treat me well. If I respect my mother, she should reciprocate. When she doesn't, the double standard irks me. I feel cheated, which can create resentment and, if allowed to fester, antagonism. For her to get respect, she has to give respect, or so my thinking goes.

The parent-child connection is among the tightest. Yet it can foster peak ambivalence or mixed emotions. On one hand, we love our kids with an intensity unimagined pre-parenthood. On the other hand, they can provoke us to such a degree that anyone peering through our window would wonder which one of us is the child. Many are the parent who confesses to me that she talks meaner to her children than to anyone. If she spoke with that same edge toward any adult, well, she'd be spending more time with her kids, as they'd be the only ones left talking to her.

Let's revisit our discipline-distressed parent. Not only is she flummoxed by her child's disobedience, but she's dismayed by her own trip-switch reactions. It's taking less to irritate her more. Before kids she thought herself pretty nice. After kids she thinks she's neither pretty nor nice.

Mom believes her accelerating anger is tethered to her child's defiance. If only Will were more cooperative, she would be more pleasant. In theory that's true. In reality it runs straight into a wall: Will. He is not about to cooperate. Mom will have to make that happen, in the process toning down her own frustration.

Mom can adjust her perception. Does this mean she should delude herself into thinking Will is really just a misunderstood sweetheart? No, it means that she should see him as a normal kid and, as such, bent toward willfulness and self-interest. Put another way, it is in Will's nature to misbehave. The closer Mom's perception is to that reality, the more calmly she can respond when the reality fights her.

Mom can depersonalize Will's behavior. Contrary to what she might think, he is not acting badly just to rattle her maternal self-image. Most kids most of the time don't deliberately set out to perturb parents. Their foremost aim is to do what they'd like, and if a parent gets upset in the process, well, that's a bonus. The parent who believes, "This is aimed at me," not only risks over-interpretation of a child's misconduct but also talks herself into more distress.

Mom can act before her self-composure departs. A standard cycle: Parent asks, tells, reminds, re-reminds, raises volume, threatens, yells. Child ignores, negotiates, argues, misbehaves more. Taking anywhere from a few minutes to a few hours to run its course, the cycle can yank a parent's emotional temperature from 98.6 degrees to 102. Had Mom disciplined rather than over-talked back at 99 degrees, her anger wouldn't have heated itself into combustion. She also would have gotten more cooperation.

Who else do we love lots? For most married couples it's our spouse. In solid marriages friction doesn't revolve so much around ever new, ever changing domestic differences. Instead a relatively small handful of ever present annoyances cause friction well beyond their size. Some universals are tardiness, strewn possessions, chore procrastination, remote control clinging, toilet lid position. A marital peeve can retain its power to provoke despite heavy efforts to persuade, plead, or bicker it away. It can take on a lifespan of years, decades even.

Once again, the thinking drifts toward personalization. "Why can't she change even a little to please me?" The seemingly intransigent, irksome habits are taken as signs that one spouse just doesn't think it's important to move one inch toward the other. When a spouse won't budge even though he's been asked and asked, what does that say about his regard for the other?

This is the question that nags many into a resentful attitude. Every twenty or thirty socks picked up adds one more emotional sock to the marriage.

How long then is long enough? When does one cease pleading and protesting? After a year? A decade? A lifetime? When does frustration get settled by an attitude that says, "I'd better learn to live with this, or at least overlook it a little, or I'll re-perturb myself every time it happens."

If this attitude is equated with a surrender of one's rights, at best it will linger only until the next irksome episode. If instead it is a healthy acceptance of what is and has been, eventually it will supplant the irritation.

My wife, Randi, is masterful at adapting herself to my domestic quirks. She is an expert organizer, structuring her days well in advance. I, on the other hand, am less structured—I like to think myself spontaneous. Thus, periodically, I fling a wrench into her schedule with something like, "Let's go out to breakfast," or, "Want to stay up and watch a movie?"

In Randi's early motherhood my proposals were unexpected add-ons, potential complications in an already overloaded agenda. With time she learned to flow with my reflex requests. And to this day she'll generally head out to breakfast with me—if I beg. Though she still falls asleep about twelve minutes into a movie.

Long-married couples, when asked about the keys to their durability, routinely answer, "We've learned to accept who the other is." They don't mean rolling over in the face of manipulation or demands. They mean tolerating the more benign foibles of personality. For while the major marriage wreckers get the most attention, day in and day out it is the minor stuff that, if allowed, can build to major discord.

Another cliché with a hard nugget of truth: You only hurt the ones you love. Perhaps it is better said, "You hurt more the ones you love, and they you." The deep investment of our feelings, indeed our very selves, in another, young or old, is what renders us most susceptible to disappointment and anger seldom experienced elsewhere.

If the mail carrier shows up two hours late, I may not like it, but I doubt I'd get bothered enough to confront him. If my teen shows up two hours late, much more is at stake—my house rules, my authority, her willingness to cooperate, her safety. Any of these dwarfs late mail in importance. The relationship is direct: The more invested my love, the stronger I react to its being ignored or mishandled.

So what do you do? Limit contact with those who fuel or feel your anger? Ask your child to find an apartment when he reaches six—somewhere in the next county? Ask your husband to live in the garage, entering the house twice a day for meals—and no talking while eating? Ask your mother-in-law to skip the next family get-together or, if she does insist on coming, to stay at least two rooms from you?

Theoretically these would eliminate interpersonal rough spots. They would also eliminate the priceless positives of close relationships. The route to living more calmly lies not at the top of the Himalayan Mountains but in learning to live with people down here.

More ideas for doing that are pages away. Don't move into the shed just yet.

TURNING THE PAGE...

We don't always act well toward those closest to us. That does not mean we're emotional misfits. Emotions that are tightly yoked to a loved one elicit not only our best but sometimes our worst. And that holds true whether our emotions are right or wrong.

Chapter Seven

. . . .

RIGHT or WRONG?

. . . .

When I attended graduate school in the '70s—the 1970s, not 1870s, as my children think—feelings covered the counseling landscape. We learned to listen empathetically and connect emotionally. We identified feelings, shared feelings, and accepted feelings. The psycho-cliché "I hear where you're coming from" could just as well acknowledge someone's unspoken emotions as his spoken words.

A popular Christian evangelist asks, "How does one reach a people who hear with their eyes and think with their feelings?"[1] In many forms of counseling, feelings are the second language. They "forge a channel" to the psyche and its workings. How someone feels, if it is to be challenged at all, is to be challenged ever so delicately, lest one demean his very personhood.

For the most part, the thinking goes, if emotions stay within appropriate social boundaries (a fuzzy assessment), any behavior they motivate is to be analyzed and understood, not necessarily confronted. The risk is that the behavior too can be assessed as acceptable, given the acceptable emotion underlying it.

A mantra repeated in grad school was "Feelings are neither good nor bad; they just are." Merely because I experience an emotion, that emotion is legitimate. To use psycho-trendy language, the emotion is "an authentic manifestation of my personal reality." While thinking is prone to misconceptions and logical errors, feelings are not so readily misleading. Since they emanate from the deeper self, to question their validity is counter therapeutic.

This mindset jetted from the halls of academia to the wider world. In a scene from a top-rated television sitcom in the 1990s, the wife is upset because her husband made jokes about her amateurish foray into the field of crafts. She tells him, "I felt humiliated." He counters that all was meant in fun and that she shouldn't feel that way. [2]

"Don't tell me how to feel," she admonishes.

His reply, "But you're wrong."

Her re-reply: "There's no right or wrong, this is how I feel."

Apparently the writers had some psychology classes in college.

To be sure, feelings flow through, in, and around us. To have no feelings whatsoever is one sign of a seriously disturbed personality. But even as a rookie psychologist, the notion that feelings just are struck me as, in a word, wrong.

An oak tree isn't right or wrong. It's just an oak tree. The sun is neither right nor wrong. It's the sun. My face is neither right nor wrong. It just is. (OK, maybe a bad example.) To place the same moral neutrality on emotions, which powerfully move behavior, seems to be stretching nonjudgmentalism too far.

My college years began in engineering. The basics of engineer-think only bolstered my leanings toward logic and analysis. My emotions, I reasoned, were marked by a fluid coming and going.

My thoughts were more stable across circumstances and generally provided a more reliable guide for my conduct.

When my counseling classes introduced me to heavy feeling-think, I listened with a raised eyebrow. The prioritizing of emotional experience just didn't feel good to me, particularly when it overshadowed qualities every bit as human, like intellect, reason, and will.

The cardinal sins—those seven human proclivities for centuries recognized as underlying much wrong conduct—include such feelings as envy, lust, and anger. Do these need to be redefined as neutral options, neither right nor wrong? Why are they still called sins? Such an out-of-date word, not to mention a negative one.

Recall simmering and silent anger. They may not always take verbal or physical shape, yet they gurgle, creating their own internal scars. At one level their wrongness is not outwardly manifest. At another it is inwardly destructive.

If my silent anger toward you mutates into hatred, is this new, fiercer feeling wrong? Suppose I'd like to hit you hard, but I never would because of legal repercussions. The desire is present; the only thing restraining its expression is fear. Is the desire wrong?

Jesus warned about sins of the heart, those feelings we accept and nurture with no attached bad conduct. He called them as wrong as the wrongful actions themselves (see Matthew 5:21–22, 27–28). Maybe he was absent the day they covered feelings in Hebrew Counseling 101.

A husband who feels lust for other women would not reassure his wife with "I see my lust as something that is authentically me. And I need to accept it—so should you—as long as it stays a desire and I don't act on it." Would she feel better after he owned the lust? Or would she wonder when and where the feelings might turn to action, despite what he says?

In return she confesses to him, "I hold a lot of bitterness toward you. But don't worry, I've come to realize that it is an integral part of my own makeup." Would he console himself with "Well, she has a right to her feelings. I have to respect that and help her, and me, live with them." Or would he be rocked by the revelation?

Whenever I feel envy or jealousy, it's not pleasant; it's unsettling. When I endure guilt over behavior that objectively isn't guilt worthy, I don't like it. And all too often, letting my temper lead me leads me to other feelings—sadness, remorse, embarrassment.

It is intuitive that some feelings help people live better and some don't. And my whole experience as a therapist confirms this.

Someone comes to therapy swirling in a cauldron of agitation and depression. She and I sort through her distress. What thoughts are fueling her feelings? What does she believe about herself because of her emotions? What behaviors do they provoke?

While we acknowledge her every emotion, and don't demean her for having them, we still recognize that they are problems. Yes, they are fully and deeply hers, but that doesn't mean they're without ill effects. Put another way, they are wrong ways to live; they don't make for a contented life.

Since this book is about anger, we can ask, "Is anger neither right nor wrong, good nor bad? If it stays confined to the inner self, does it thereby lie beyond the reach of moral or social scrutiny? In short, is anger a feeling that just is?"

The answer lies on two levels. At a base level, anger just is. No one is without some measure of it—even my Aunt Esther. Often it's a semiautomatic physiological reaction to a perceived insult or threat—a harsh word, provocative situation, nasty person. To call the reaction wrong would be misleading. The instantaneous internal flare, devoid of misconduct, isn't necessarily wrong. It just is, or more precisely, it just happens.

Occasionally someone will send me a hostile e-mail over something I've said at a presentation. My knee-jerk reaction might be indignation, and depending upon how long I dwell upon the injustice, it could swell into retaliation. If, however, I settle my insides or, more typically, allow my wife to settle them for me, am I doing anything wrong?

While reflexively I felt anger, it didn't control me. I controlled it. The ideal would be that I not get so upset in the first place, but what am I? A psychologist or something?

The level above feeling, that of expression, is where most of us live. That is, how does my anger show itself? In ways that are helpful or hurtful? And what is the ratio of helpful to hurtful?

A fantasy: My wife accuses me of overreacting, and in my mind I respond with, "I'm so mad I can't think straight. She's going to get a heartfelt thank you letter for so clearly pointing out my flaws. And if she keeps up the accusations, I'm going to write a check to her favorite charity. I'll show her."

Here my anger leads to nothing negative. Just the opposite: It leads to positive, assuming I do write the letter or check. But first I have to calm down.

The reality: Angry reactions are typically more hurtful than helpful. The emotion itself may be psychologically understandable; nonetheless, it is regularly so bound to overheated words or behavior that the whole package could be called bad. A fundamental social law: The harsher the emotion, the more it drags with it regrettable repercussions.

Driving a car ninety miles per hour would not be inherently wrong if accompanied by a guarantee that no one and nothing would be hurt and providing it were legal, as on the autobahn. Ninety miles per hour is not the problem—that's crawling on a stock car racetrack. The problem is the risk that travels with that speed anywhere else.

Let's say I were able to completely, always and everywhere, divorce my feeling-anger from any action-anger. The feeling is moving within me but not toward anyone else. One could argue, I suppose, that the feeling alone is less wrong than one coupled with nasty conduct. Who is able, though, to operate consistently in such a split state of mind? It would seem both a physical and psychological impossibility.

Were I to return to graduate school today and hear "feelings just are," I'm not sure I could sit quietly in skepticism. I'd likely feel compelled to ask, "If a feeling routinely provokes behavior that is bad, can we legitimately label that feeling neutral?"

And that is why, in addition to my flagrant use of value judgment language (such as *bad*), I now would struggle to pass a few of those courses.

TURNING THE PAGE...

Any emotion can be considered a piece of humanness that just is. That doesn't render it unanswerable to moral judgment. Some feelings are more troublesome than others. Some are wrong in themselves, and some have great potential to lead to wrongful conduct.

Anger, however, doesn't always lead to unwanted behavior. Depending upon its context, anger can be an ally or an adversary.

Chapter Eight

· · · · · · ·

ALLY or ADVERSARY?

· · · · · · ·

Anger suffers from image problems. It's safe to call this an understatement. In most people's minds, anger is solidly yoked to some unsavory partners—screaming, cursing, put-downs, aggression, violence. And that's the short list. But anger is not a through-and-through bad guy. It does have some redeeming qualities.

Psychoanalysis uses something called a word association test. The analyst says a word, for example, *mother*, and the patient offers the first word to enter his head. Theoretically the spontaneous response will slip past any inhibitions to reveal forbidden feelings the patient has about his mother, thereby opening for the analyst a look into his more real and more raw inner self.

I'm not a psychoanalyst, but let's conduct our own word association test. Suppose I say "anger," what would you say? It's not "mother," is it? For most people, words like *rage, assault, hostile,* or *mean* would jump out. The answers would be clustered around words with reputations as poor as anger's.

How likely would I be to hear "helpful, motivating, determined"? None of these are routinely coupled to an emotion with

PRACTICAL SOLUTIONS FOR CONQUERING ANGER

so much potential to spur poor behavior. Yet if governed, anger can be an ally.

Emotions motivate. Exactly what they motivate depends upon how much the mind and will work side by side as partners.

Anger ranks high on the list of emotion motivators (emotivators?). Along with fear, it is wired into us as part of a physiological chain reaction that is the body's defense in the service of survival. Biologists call it the fight or flight response. (Note which word is first.) When the mind senses danger, it orders the body to marshal its resources for immediate and focused action.

For us moderns, the threats are not so much physical as social and interpersonal. Sometimes we fight—argue, yell, react. Sometimes we flee—yield, withdraw, shut down. And there is a third response: It is to do what one should do. We could call this "fight or flight or right."

Anger can be likened to a horse. The smallest horse can pull more than a human. Get a bit into that horse's mouth, and even the biggest one can use its strength for our purposes.

For nearly forty years I have lifted weights. A law of the gym—grounded in gravity and body physics—is that the first set of an exercise is a lifter's strongest. Because he is muscle fresh, he can push his maximum repetitions. Added sets will see lower numbers—either less repetitions or less weight, sometimes both.

About 95 percent of the time, this law rules my lifting. The other 5 percent I break the law, lifting stronger on my second set. Why so? Determination stoked by anger.

Occasionally, for whatever reason—bad form, distraction, too much talking instead of lifting—I have a weak first set, resulting in frustration at my poor performance. Rather than fuming and stomping around, however, I've learned to channel the resulting frustration, using it to my lifting advantage. I can convert my physiological state into performance. And after a better second set, the frustration dissipates quickly. I'm pleased again, until the next bad set.

An extreme display of anger strength is seen with the five foot, two inch, 120-pound woman who hoists a tipped lawn tractor or even a car off her pinned husband or child. She knows she can't budge that weight, but her "I have to do something" surge overcomes all other reactions of the moment, emotional and physical. Though her first response may be fear, it is rapidly replaced by a body-altering drive. One could say her strength peaks during her first weightlifting try.

A common parent-child scenario: A thirteen-year-old has been nagging for a cell phone since preschool. OK, I exaggerate—since first grade. Up to now Mom has stood fast, having multiple reasons not to connect her daughter to the whole Western Hemisphere. But she wears down, finally caving to peer pressure, her daughter's pestering, and logistics. (Well, the daughter does need to call when practice is over.) Mom's instincts are anti-phone, yet she suppresses them and gives up the cell.

In short time daughter and phone confirm all Mom's misgivings. Mom is forced to conclude the phone was a bad call, but she still is reluctant to pull its plug—I mean, charger. After a string of her daughter's misuses crammed into one week, however, Mom has had enough. Her frustration over being manipulated finally moves her to do what she wanted to do back when—hang up the phone. In the end she needed an emotional prod to do the right thing—as she judged, anyway.

Anger can be a tool in the counselor's office. One wouldn't think that a venue for lowering emotional thermostats could employ anger as a therapeutic technique. But it can.

In the 1980s a high-profile condition was called agoraphobia, from a Greek word meaning "fear of the marketplace." The official diagnosis now is generalized anxiety disorder. It refers to a crippling level of fear in a range of everyday places—a store, a crowd, a restaurant, a car.

A sense of impending panic follows an anxious individual. Psychologists call it anticipatory anxiety. In shirt-sleeve talk it's the fear of being afraid. The anxiety lurks at a low level, always ready to assert itself in the person's mind. Not only does this constrict her social movement, but it also pushes her to run from places she once enjoyed.

Standard treatment consists of a step-by-step exposure to the dreaded circumstances, either in the client's imagination or in real life. The goal is to teach her to exchange her anxiety for relaxation. Simply put, it is hard to feel anxious when one is relaxed.

A second strategy uses an opposing physical state: anger. Anger too is a state hostile to fear. Simply put, it is hard to feel anxious when one is angry. If an individual can foster the attitude "I refuse to be mastered by this anxiety," the anxiety will leave her one place at a time.

When counseling someone nervous about eating in a restaurant or about driving, I might ask, "Do you like being controlled by your anxiety?"

"No, not at all."

"Does it frustrate you that the thinking you is being dominated by the feeling you?"

"If I dwell on it, it does."

"Can you dwell on this frustration with a purpose? Can you use it to increase your resolve?" The aim is to energize the client to conquer the anxiety.

A colleague described the case of a businessman who had developed a debilitating dread of elevators after having an unexplained panic attack in one. Because he did business in tall buildings, his career was definitely threatened. As counseling untangled the mechanics of the attack, he grew more incensed over how his mind had duped his body. Being a take-charge sort, he paid someone to operate an elevator, continuously hauling him up and down while he overrode his fear. He used his anger at himself for social and career gain. (Maybe he also figured paying an elevator operator was cheaper than paying a therapist.)

Early in my graduate school days, other students warned me about a professor who could be intimidating. Wouldn't you know it, he became my supervisor, and I was uptight —more due to his reputation than to his actual conduct. With each meeting I became more upset about my being upset around him. Why was I allowing this? My reaction to him was foolish.

I found a technique to overcome my distress: I got mad at it. When my anger at me got greater than my unease around him, I settled in his presence. My supervisor, had he known, would have been proud.

Can anger be a proper, even moral, response? Should we feel some incense at seeing another mistreated or at witnessing an injustice?

The Bible recounts a scene where Jesus enters the Jerusalem temple and confronts moneychangers who are using the crowded worship space for their own profit. Reacting with a protective zeal for his Father's house, Jesus overturns the tables and drives out the merchants (see Matthew 21:12–13). Was his anger inappropriate? Should Jesus have kept his anger to himself?

Christians believe that Jesus is God in the flesh. He demonstrated the fact that anger directed properly can be a social and moral good.

If anger has upsides, why do its downsides get most of the attention? Because anger resists moderation. Like a microphone placed too near its speaker, a feedback loop is formed, marked by escalating volume and pitch. When we can marshal its power, anger is an ally.

Anger must answer to us, not us to it, or it will become an adversary.

TURNING THE PAGE...

The saying is, Sometimes a vice is just a virtue carried to an extreme. We can say about anger, "Sometimes this vice can be a virtue if not taken to an extreme."

Still, not every benefit of anger is good for you. It depends on whether your gain is primary or secondary.

Chapter Nine

. . . .

PRIMARY or SECONDARY?

. . . .

There is a concept in psychology called secondary gain. It has its roots in old Freudian theory. According to Freud, psychiatric symptoms have a primary purpose: to reduce conflict in one's unconscious mind. Often, however, they assume a second purpose: to gain some sort of social benefit.

Though most clinicians no longer see the mind through Freud's eyes, secondary gain has settled into their vision. It now refers to whatever reinforces the persistence of troublesome behaviors and emotions.

To illustrate, long about mid-October an adolescent girl develops vague stomach complaints for which no physical cause can be identified. The primary gain looks to be the avoidance of school or, more narrowly, someone or something there. As her sick days at home accumulate, a secondary gain—hours at the computer—also accumulates. Her bellyaches started with her school resistance. The perks of home only served to further upset her stomach at the thought of school.

Consider an adult with a history of drug abuse. Somewhere in his years-long up-and-down battle to overcome the pull of chemicals, he becomes eligible for public assistance, provided he enters counseling. Whereupon his therapeutic picture becomes complicated by a financial factor: the loss of income that could result from too much improvement.

For both individuals, what began as behavior bringing trouble evolved into behavior bringing benefit too. Life is full of such mixed-motive conduct or, as the psychologists call it, ambivalence.

It's an often-asked question: "If my emotions are causing me or others so much pain, why is it so hard for me to overcome them?" Lots of answers to that query, but one is, "You may be gaining something in the midst of what you're losing."

Anger can carry a secondary gain. Parents will confess, "I have to get mad, then he listens." Clearly they are bothered at needing to reach jackhammer volume, complete with agitation, to get heard. Yet they are rewarded, part of the time anyway, with some compliance. So they have come to accept—perhaps a better word is *endure*—the need to exchange bad temper for good behavior, though the exchange rate is not always one to one. Sometimes lots of anger reaps little obedience.

In therapy a wife will disclose, "The only time my husband will listen to my side is when I get really upset."

"What happens if you give your side without getting upset?"

"He doesn't take me seriously. He thinks I like to complain."

"Is this because he needs a certain level of volume to pay attention, or because you've trained him to hear you only when you're riled?"

"I think I must have trained him. He wasn't so much this way earlier in our marriage."

"How many times do you think you can keep getting upset before you lose credibility?"

"That's already happening. I'm seen as the emotional lunatic. The look I get is, 'Here she goes again.'"

One feature of an addiction is habituation, or tolerance. Over time more of something—in frequency or intensity—is needed to produce a similar reaction. What once provided a kick has lost potency. Further, the earlier dosage no longer does much of anything other than forestall a painful crash or withdrawal.

Something similar is true with anger. Let's return to our high-decibel parent. Yes, adding volume to his words does afford them some emotional oomph—initially. It sends a loud message: "Now, I mean it!" If anger characterizes a parent's style, however, a child will habituate to it. The more he learns that no action will occur until Mom or Dad flares, the less heed he will pay until she or he does. The parent is then required to add even more emotional *drug* to get a response. It's an unhealthy cycle for parent and child.

No question, enlisting anger for social advantage can be seductive. Anger can control, manipulate, intimidate. A spouse with a temper can make his wife and children stay out of his way when he's in that mood. A friend with an ever-prickly reaction to honest disagreement will teach others to keep opinions inside when around him.

In the short term, anger can obtain for someone what he wants: to win the argument, to be left alone, to get cooperation. But how often can he so succeed without being branded as mean, or unfair, or unreasonable, or just plain babyish? Anger is a harsh master:

The more you win with it, the more you lose.

Anger may force a change in another's behavior; it's unlikely to change his mind or heart. Children intimidated by a parent's erratic eruptions may comply, but they aren't likely to internalize their compliance. The attitude hardens: "I'll learn not to provoke you, but I won't learn to respect you."

A rage may end an argument with a spouse; it won't end the disagreement. It may scream another into silence; it won't lead him to agree. With repetition, anger can deaden another's motivation to seek the real cause of that anger.

Should your aim be never to rely on anger in any circumstances? I wouldn't advise that.

First, who can never get angry? That's an unrealistic ambition. You'll just get mad at yourself whenever you fail.

Second, anger is like a spice. If not overused, it can add flavor to your message. The parent who gets uncharacteristically distressed over his child's misconduct speaks emphatically: "I see what you did as serious." Many parents recall, "My dad (mom) seldom got very angry with me, but when he (she) did, I knew I had crossed a line. And it was a good lesson, one I never forgot."

Once my son was badgering his mother for permission to go somewhere. After she refused to yield, he sought me. It's called "appealing the decision." Savvy kids use it, making experienced trial lawyers look like first-year law students.

After hearing my son out—my first mistake—I made a second, much bigger one. "Well, if it were up to me, I'd let you." Whereupon he headed back to his mother with this new piece of evidence.

The next face I saw was my wife's, a quite unhappy one. "Don't ever do that to me. You put me in the position of being the bad parent. I felt betrayed."

I should have known that. But the intensity of my wife's reaction, coming from someone not prone to such reactions, taught me well for the future: Don't ever make her look like a mean mom. As she says, she's quite capable of doing that without my help, thank you.

Strong emotion—if not spinning out of control—can convey "What you did really hurt." Or, "I'm feeling badly mistreated." Or, "You are pushing me too far." The key is that the emotion punctuates the message; it is not the message itself.

Resist using anger as a social tool. Any secondary gain may lead to a primary problem.

TURNING THE PAGE...

Anything that provides some social reward can be a temptation, no matter its social liability. You can lessen anger's social liability, however, by honestly asking, my fault or yours?

Chapter Ten

. . . .

MY FAULT or YOURS?

. . . .

Seldom does someone begin his first marriage counseling session
with, "You know why I'm here? Because I've finally realized how
difficult I am to live with. And I asked my spouse to come along
to help me take a good, hard look at myself. I want to know just
how much of our marriage problems are me."

Rather the goal is: "Fix my spouse. Make him (her) see just how
difficult he (she) is to live with. And I'm here to help you do that."

Of course, some marriages are on life support due to real difficult stuff: infidelity, abuse, pornography, gambling. More often,
though, the atmosphere has worsened little by little. The spouses
have drifted apart and quit trying, or they just plain like less and
less about the other. A line from one disgruntled movie husband
captures well the deteriorated state of the relationship: "I hate the
way she licks stamps!"[3]

In most longtime unhappy marriages, each person has a finger
pointed at the other as the chief culprit. If only he (she) were more
pleasant, or communicative, or understanding, or helpful, or
(enter adjective here), then I could be a better spouse.

This message also comes from parents. A mom or dad will call me seeking counseling for a child. Typically the call is about the child's behavior, mostly rebellious or uncooperative. Whether the child is three, nine, or sixteen, I usually say the same thing: "I don't work much with children."

"Oh?" A perplexed silence follows, then I elaborate.

"I work with the parent or parents. They are the ones to bring about the most and the quickest improvement."

Some parents acknowledge that their discipline needs reshaping: It needs to be firmer, more resolute, more consistent, kinder. Some still wonder why I prefer to work with them, as they see the main fix needs to be directed at the child, who is clearly the reason for the call.

Projecting explanation outward is among the most active of personal defenses. It guards the self, asserting that I am, on the whole, a good and decent person, or a better and more decent person than you are being, anyway. A bias inward is not some kind of neurosis. We are all wired to protect ourselves, not just physically but socially and emotionally. Thus we are slow to acknowledge our unqualified share of shared trouble.

"I'll admit I've got faults, but he's the king of faults." "I know I say things I shouldn't say sometimes, but she says a lot more and a lot more often." "I know I'm not perfect, but she…" I call it the *I-but* defense: *I* acknowledge some blame on my end, *but* the real weight sits on someone else's end."

Suppose my wife and I spend seventeen minutes in an "Oh, yeah, what about you?" reciprocating bicker fest. And suppose some psychologist (not me—my wife would object) asks us to assess our individual percentages of contrariness. I measure my wife's at 64 percent and mine at 36 percent. She says it's 69 percent me and 31 percent her. The total percentage of other-blame is 133 percent, for sure a mathematical error. Likely a personal one as well.

Whatever the numbers, both my wife and I tag the other as the main ingredient in the stew. We hear the argument and its escalation from our own personal realities.

So how close is my personal reality to reality? A fair question. Also a fairly unanswerable one. How do I objectively measure it? I may be convinced that my assessment is accurate to within plus or minus three percentage points. But again, am I the most unbiased observer of me?

How about finding unbiased observers to rate who of us is the more difficult? (That's often what spouses hope the therapist will do.) Though the raters may be more objective than either me or my wife—most certainly than my wife!—each still sees us through his own subjective lens. One may judge my three curse words more offensive than my wife's three eye rolls. Another rates her eye rolls ruder. (He must have teenagers.)

Then too, does fault fluctuate with the flow of the fracas? My scolding remark started it. My wife countered with two retorts. My voice volume leaped hers by twenty-five decibels. She calmed down, but I strained upward. Toward the end I offered a half-hearted apology, but she was only in half a mind to hear it.

Many altercations take similar form: "I wouldn't have gotten so mad if she would have quit pushing me." "I can only take so much, and then I have to defend myself." "I didn't want trouble, but he seemed to be itching for a fight." In other words, my portion of blame is lessened by how hard I was attacked.

The uglier the clash, the more I'm disposed to see you as the bigger problem. As I hear it, what I'm arguing is more legitimate than what you're arguing. My perspective makes more sense than yours. Therefore, if I get a little hot, well, that's understandable. If you were more reasonable—if you thought more as I do—I wouldn't have gotten so feisty.

A principle of Therapy 101: Our natural inclination is to play down personal responsibility for conduct, especially bad conduct. And the worse our conduct, the less our self-assigned blame. A first goal of much counseling is to help someone more accurately see his role in his reactions.

This self-preservation tendency is in panoramic view when a high-profile public figure is caught in wrongdoing. A stock apology is, "Mistakes were made." Note the passive verb: not "I made a mistake," but they were made. Note too the morally neutral word *mistake*. Not a wrong, not a moral transgression, but some type of miscalculation, as in two plus two equals five. Something within us just rebels at accepting unconditional personal responsibility. Oops, I mean, we rebel at it.

A study compared how we see our own foibles with how we see others'. It found that we tend to see our weakness as due more to specific circumstances while seeing others' as part of their personality. For example, if I trip coming down the stairs, it's because they are poorly lit, or the carpet is wrinkled, or I am in a hurry. If you trip coming down the stairs, you probably are clumsy, or careless, or inattentive. I show more tolerance for my missteps than I do for yours.

Are we psychologically checkmated? Can we seldom know without a doubt how much we're at fault in a conflict?

That might seem so. In many verbal maelstroms, the water, however clear initially, gets pretty muddy pretty fast. Yet there is a way out of the confusion. Rather than aiming to parse out who was more wrong how, suppose I accept the fact that I could be more wrong than I think? Entertaining that possibility usually puts one on safe psychological ground.

Counselors observe that many people come to therapy because they've realized that something is wrong—in their marriage, child rearing, or life. Or they've realized that something is more wrong than they had thought. It is this dawning insight that initially moves them toward more honest self-scrutiny and then on to self-betterment.

Alcoholics Anonymous asserts that someone has to hit bottom, often rock bottom, before he is ready to look clearly at himself and begin the climb upward. He must place more responsibility for his conduct into his hands and less into others'. Then and only then will he be seriously committed to change what needs to be changed.

AA warns against comparative thinking: "I'm not as bad as that guy or as bad as I could be." Pretty much any one of us can look better—or worse—depending upon whom we choose for comparison. After all, my anger is trivial when measured against that of inmates imprisoned for armed violence. Then again, how would my self-composure stack up against Gandhi's?

Because an individual seeks professional help for his anger does not necessarily mean he's angrier than those who don't seek help. How much he wants to change depends upon how much he sees his actions as hurting himself or others. It is unrelated to how much someone else might be hurting himself or others.

The Scottish poet Robert Burns wrote, "Oh, would some power the gift give us, / To see ourselves as others see us."[4] Whether I get angry little or lots, I must realize that my self-assessment is tainted by my self-protective subjectivity. While I may not always be realistic where I am involved, at least if I know I'm not always realistic, I've made a good start. I can then begin to be more objective about me.

TURNING THE PAGE...

It's not easy to admit to being wrong or to being as wrong as one is. This is particularly so when the wrongdoing is part of a pattern. And the more I feel compelled to act wrongly, the more I need to ask, "Am I master or mastered?"

Chapter Eleven

. . . .

MASTER or MASTERED?

. . . .

The 1970s comic Flip Wilson had a signature line: "The devil made me do it." Theologically speaking, the claim is faulty. Practically speaking, the claim has believers.

Many view anger, for example, as a sort of emotional demon that takes possession of them over their better nature. Bad conduct, commanded by extreme emotion, is something that, however temporarily, runs beyond the limits of their everyday self.

Parents of little children observe, "When he goes into one of his rages, it's like he's completely unreachable. Nothing we say or do can calm him down."

As a group, little people have far less developed self-control than big people. Still, despite what most parents think, most kids can be pacified rather quickly. It just takes the right incentive.

For example, a mother could say, "OK, Storm, go ahead. Do what you want. And here's a cookie to munch on to help calm you down."

Not that I'm advising such, but how fast would Storm's surge plummet? Within seconds, I suspect. Would the cookie technique work with a teen? One might need to ratchet up to the car technique.

Recall one of your worst anger displays. If you can't think of any, I have a couple of questions. One, have you mentally suppressed them out of shame? Or two, if you've never had a single one, why are you reading this book?

Perhaps your dilemma is deciding which anger display to choose. If so, pick the one that felt the most emotionally compelling, the one that seemed to put you into some kind of altered state.

Suppose, at the peak of your outburst, I were to approach you, a million-dollar money order in hand, promising, "Get control within three seconds, and this is yours." No joke, no lie, a legitimate offer, one that you believed.

Would you rage on, "Look, buddy, I'd like your money, but right now I've got a lot more inside me that needs to come out. Besides, even if I wanted to, I couldn't get a grip that fast"?

Or would you need about one second to calm down and the other two seconds to pocket the money? Would it take a million? How about $100,000? $10,000? $1,000? OK, how about ten bucks?

Whether the motivator is a cookie, a car, or cash, the point is that almost anyone can terminate a tirade if she thinks it worthwhile. The issue is one of price.

One could counter, "Sure, make the offer worth it, and I could settle. But when would I ever get such an offer?"

Perhaps not in a material sense, but how about in a personal or social sense? Here are plenty of reasons to tone it down: to save someone's feelings, not to look foolish or soak in later guilt, and to keep in check nasty, destructive, or physical stuff.

In the eighth grade, in an instant of unrestrained fury, I punched a wall and promptly broke my hand. Sometimes the cost of poor self-control dwarfs the cost of gaining self-control.

No doubt, intense emotion can feel like a compulsion, exerting its will over ours until spent. Just as our perceptions about another's inner state can be mistaken, however, so too can our perceptions about our own. More remnants of self-control lie within than we think. The question is not, "Can I control me if given good enough reason?" The question is, "Can I control me?" In most circumstances the answer is yes.

In any heated situation, underestimating the reservoir of self-control reflects repetition. Meaning, the more I've acted with similar anger in similar circumstances, the more it feels as if something within me takes over, rendering me, if not helpless to the emotion, at least dragged along by it. After all, it's happened so many times that it just seems like an unthinking reflex.

It may seem so, but it's not. My reaction, no matter how immediate, is not fully automatic. It may be a long-standing habit, but it's not a mindless reflex. As long as my brain is operating, I still have resources to counter my impulses.

Then too, exerting my thinking brain over my emotional brain takes less energy in the beginning moments of a tirade than at its midpoint or its full-blown extreme. Braking a runaway freight train is nearly impossible. The brakes will burn out, leaving the train to stop only after it crashes into something. Slamming on the brakes early in the train's momentum is far more likely to slow it to a stop. And the earlier done the easier.

Runaway emotions don't launch at peak speed. Little kids, well known for their limited self-restraint, don't typically roar from zero to sixty in two seconds. Their frustration gathers energy. A cookie offered to stop a fit at the three-second mark might not need to be as big as one offered at thirty-three seconds. At the three-minute mark, though, even the biggest double-stuffed, chocolate-coated Oreo might have trouble chewing its way through the turbulence.

Likewise, once a grown-up tantrum has reached its apex, the absence of self-control can feel all too real. However, "I can't control myself" is often just another way of saying, "When I'm out of control, I can't control myself." In reality the descent toward no restraint is not without opportunity for some restraint along the way.

Have you ever thought, "I'd better leave now, before I say or do something I'll regret"? You knew to hit the road before reaching a point of emotional no return. You acted smartly before losing more capacity to act smartly.

Basketball has taught me that lesson repeatedly. The game is a prime court for flare-ups. It's fast paced, with ten bodies pushing and slamming against one another—accidentally or deliberately. Over years of pickup games, I've developed a skill more valuable than a left-hand hook shot: knowing when to pull myself from a game for a needed emotional breather. As my frustration goes up, I sit down. Not acting stupid is much easier if, early in my drive toward stupid, I take charge of my body—more particularly, my testosterone stuff of competition.

"I can't control myself" can mean "I don't want to control myself." Super-charged emotions can sustain an attitude of "I'm angry, I deserve to be, and I have little intent to hold back." The problem may not be so much a loss of ability to master oneself but the lack of will to do so. And anytime one's will is compromised, it is that much more swiftly overpowered by galloping emotions. More intense outbursts can come with an unexpected partner: "I'm so mad, I don't care what I do or say." It's pretty predictable: The more anger, the less thought given to the consequences. Only later, when the raw emotion has subsided, do other emotions follow: guilt, shame, embarrassment, regret. Intense emotion dampens the concern for how one is acting. But just as the emotion slowly leaves, so too does the sense of apathy. Then we are left to care how we acted.

Few really believe that "the devil made me do it." Still, many are inclined to attach blame to someone or something outside themselves—a provocation, insult, personal attack, basketball game. When all the dust settles, however, the most accurate belief about an angry display is, "I made me do it."

TURNING THE PAGE...

Not much in life can truly make us do anything; not much can force our emotions. Influences, situations, and people can coax, even draw out, the worst in us. Still, the final determination to keep going or to pull back lies within our power. Recognizing so will help us determine whether our reaction is a right or a choice.

Chapter Twelve

. . . .

A RIGHT or A CHOICE?

. . . .

Many parents today decry their youngster's attitude of entitlement. Social freedoms and material goodies, in the child's eyes, are not privileges to be gained by growing up responsibly; they are rights that accrue simply because she has reached a magic age, because her peers have them, or because she breathes.

An exercise I offer parents: When you next discipline by revoking some privilege—cell phone, computer, driving, dating, sleeping past noon—observe closely your child's sense of victimization. The intensity of her reaction is closely connected to how much she believes you are stealing from her not a generously granted favor but a God-given due of youthful existence.

Not only the young react severely when denied something seen as rightfully theirs. It can be disappointing or frustrating to lose a bonus. It can be downright infuriating not to possess what is considered a deserved possession. The natural course of an ever-accessible benefit is toward a perceived right.

In my boyhood neither our house nor our car had air conditioning. Nor did most of our neighbors'. We weren't poor; we were typical. Not until I was nearing college did my parents install a box air conditioner in our family room. (Looking back, their timing is suspicious.) On sweltering August nights, we congregated in that room, appreciative of the temperature inside.

Today it is nearly unthinkable that any new home or car would not come with air conditioning standard. Cool air is expected. My kids whine when piling into our van in the summertime, "Dad, turn on the air." I never thought anything could preempt "Tell him to quit looking at me."

When I was in high school—I'm starting more sentences as my father would—only a handful of my classmates drove to school. Most of us rode the buses. They were no-cost, reasonably safe, and supervised.

Some twenty or so years ago, teens around the country started a new student movement. (How they all so quickly coalesced, prior to texting and Facebook, baffles me.) High school seniors decided that the bus was beneath them. It was relegated to the vehicle of lower classmates and the more transportationally uncool upper ones. Any senior worth the rank would drive to school, alone or with friends.

While sharing with me their exasperation over this teen tsunami, most parents were reluctant to challenge it, not wanting to ride against their youngster's resistance. At the time I asked, "How long before the juniors, even sophomores, seek the same privilege-turned-demand?" Currently this is the scene. The bus is now the last resort for high schoolers. A perk of seniority morphed into an immovable right of passage.

What does all this social evolution have to do with anger? Most people don't regard anger as some kind of privilege. True, but many do consider it some kind of right, especially in response to a repeated offense. Their strong emotion may have once been a choice, but with time and re-offense, it assumes unquestioned status.

"After all she's done to me, I have every right to be upset." "I have the right to tell him exactly how I feel." "She had no right to act that way." In effect, "I have a right to my anger." And that right is beyond dispute. It is more than allowed; it is a given.

This mindset is not to be confused with what an earlier chapter called righteous anger. Risking oversimplification, righteous anger follows an injustice or harm done to another, while right-filled anger tends to wrap around a wrong done to oneself. The wrong may be real or imagined, but the anger around it feels quite justified.

The 1970s saw the birth of a quasi-therapy called assertiveness training. A.T. rapidly asserted itself both inside and outside the universities, with no shortage of big-selling books piggybacking on its momentum (*Looking Out for #1*). A.T. taught the emotional necessity to firmly, but not aggressively, assert one's rights in social settings and relationships. To ignore those rights would be to invite resentments and, in the extreme, to risk becoming an emotional basket case.

By its nature assertiveness is an animal tough to tame. If allowed a long leash, it can be trained into pushiness. Through an ever more sensitive vigilance for any offense, however slight, I can assert myself into obnoxiousness. In teaching others never to walk on me, I can teach them to walk way around me. Sometimes it is healthier, for both the slighter and the slighted, to let some things pass.

In ancient Middle Eastern cultures, a slap on the cheek was taken as a severe personal insult. Jesus counseled, "If any one strikes you on the right cheek, turn to him the other also" (Matthew 5:39). In other words, don't reflexively feel insulted. Show the offender that his scorn can't provoke you to retaliatory wrath. Maybe Jesus missed the Assertiveness 101 course in synagogue.

Psychology, whether recognizing so or not, regularly comes alongside biblical wisdom. One survey concluded that those who turn the other cheek, not from cowardice but from confidence, are less prickly and more content in their relationships. By setting aside some of their rights, they are emotionally more settled rather than less. Just the opposite of assertiveness training.

A sense of right-full anger can climb along a number of paths. It can ascend from a feeling of innocence: "I didn't do anything to deserve that treatment." Perhaps not.

Perhaps you are the target of an inexplicable, surprising act of meanness. Such is the nature of much mistreatment. To feel unjustly assailed is understandable. And the greater the injustice, the worse it feels.

Still, to hold tight to my right to be treated well, when I have done little or nothing to provoke anyone, is asking for distress. A powerful, nearly immutable social law is: You can't *make* others act right, no matter how good you are to them. You can ask for good treatment, persuade, plead for it, but you can't demand it. Demand it, out loud or in your mind, and a strong sense of grievance follows if you don't receive it.

Also at work is the law of social reciprocation: I treat you well; you should respond in kind. I have earned your good will, especially if you are someone close to me—spouse, mother, child, coworker. The scale should be balanced or at least not too slanted. As we have observed elsewhere, the very closeness of a relationship brings with it more opportunities for misunderstanding and friction. Emotional ties do tighten with mutual regard. On this side of heaven, though, in most relationships, one person gives more than the other. If you are that person, know that you are doing right, even when your rights are ignored. Such is the fluctuating, give-and-take nature of even the best relationships.

"Your behavior cost me"—time, money, reputation, sleep. Anything I lose because of your actions gives me ample cause to be incensed. Few would argue my loss. Fewer would disagree with my emotions about it. Nonetheless, how much right-filled anger will it take to bring back my time, money, reputation, or sleep? The anger will only add another cost—my peace of mind.

Whatever satisfaction I might gain by soaking in my justified anger will be more than offset by my prolonged irritation. The sooner I can let it go, the sooner I will cut my losses. In the words of the song, "You got to know when to hold 'em, know when to fold 'em."[5]

How do I know how much right I have to be aggrieved? The determination is a tricky one. I may feel I have the right, but over and over we've seen how feelings can mislead. In themselves they are not the most reliable guides to conduct.

My anger over a bad situation may be among the most intense feelings I've ever had. That doesn't mean the feeling is grounded in a right reading of reality. My sizing up of the situation may be slanted or incomplete.

What if the real wrong done to me is a perceived wrong? I may be convinced that my wife just undercut my discipline by telling my son, "Sure," not ten minutes after I told him, "Absolutely not." And I may be itching to confront her, only to hear that she knew nothing about my ruling, as my son conveniently neglected to mention it. I got myself all distressed up with no place to go. Until I find my son, that is.

Suppose I ask a hundred people, "Do I have the right to be angry given what was done to me?" And suppose eighty-two of them answer, "Yes. I know I would." Other than feeling justified by consensus, what do these poll results do for me? How does that right help me or another?

Of course, I can tell the offender exactly how I feel if my main goal is to air my feelings. If my main goal is to smooth the relationship, however, I must first ask myself, "How likely is he to see it all my way and to gratefully accept my assertiveness?" My right to speak my mind may actually cause more friction between us, as it serves more fodder for offense, for both of us. Assertiveness must always be tempered by hefty doses of good judgment.

Occasionally someone will send me an e-mail blistering me for something I said somewhere. My temptation to blister back can be fierce. Do I have a right to respond?

Most people would probably say, "No doubt. Go for it," especially if they read the e-mail. But what purpose would my right serve? The longer I contemplate when and how I might answer, the longer my agitation stays with me. Further, any but the most apologetic return e-mail could trigger a nastier re-mail. From both responding and not, I've learned that anger fades more quickly if I turn the other cheek, cyber speaking, that is.

The old saw observes, "I had the right of way, but it did me no good. The bus still hit my car." Put another way, "I was in the right, but I got hurt anyway."

TURNING THE PAGE...

Sometimes "I have a right" is another way of saying "I want to."

The country song goes, "You can feel bad if it makes you feel better."[6] Managing anger is best viewed as a choice. Anger is, if you will, a privilege, for good or ill. Give it the status of a right, and you make it immune to scrutiny.

Of course, just because something is a right doesn't make it right. It is always good to ask: Is my normal anger right?

Chapter Thirteen

· · · · · · ·

NORMAL or RIGHT?

· · · · · · ·

A stepmom expressed to me her surging frustration over the kids' mother's mean-spirited undercutting of her own relationship with the children. Because she saw little hope of a decrease in manipulations, she asked in exasperation, "Isn't it normal to feel the way I feel? Wouldn't anybody?"

When I asked her why she asked that, she replied, "At least I'd know I'm not nuts."

"Well," I said, "you're not. But you still are letting her get to you almost daily. And that is driving you nuts."

With the relentless psychologizing of society, "Is it normal?" has emerged as the question du jour. It occupies a high rung on the ladder of life's inquiries. Feelings are judged by it: "I think almost everybody else would feel as I do." As is behavior: "Who wouldn't do what I did under the circumstances?"

"It's normal" follows not far behind "It's my right." After all, if I have the right, so do others. And the more others there are who exercise that right, the more normal we all are.

Call it anger by the numbers. My anger is more understandable, acceptable even, if I know others would react as I do. The axiom is, "Misery loves company."

Perhaps other stepparents would react as my client did were they in her shoes—or house. Stepmom may take some consolation in knowing that she's not alone in her frustration. But how does that help her? She'll feel the same whether twenty or two hundred other parents share her misery.

The critical question is not "Is it normal?" Much self-frustrating behavior is normal, in the sense that plenty of people do likewise. The critical question is, "Is it good?"

Less than 5 percent of the population would score above 130 on a standard IQ test. An IQ of 130 is not normal, if you will. Yet most people would want an IQ of 130—especially parents, whose IQs drift further downward with each child. At the least, an IQ of 130 improves career options.

Even if less than 5 percent of people would react as calmly as you when provoked, would people refuse your capacity for self-control if offered to them? "No, thank you. I like feeling so agitated. At least I feel more normal."

Normal and good sit on two different planes. What is normal is not necessarily good. And what is good is not necessarily normal.

Bishop Fulton Sheen, who had a popular Catholic television show in the 1950s, said, "Right is right even if nobody is right; and wrong is wrong if everybody is wrong."[7] Good is not judged by consensus, no matter how uniform the consensus.

Suppose my reaction is extreme—plainly wrong, plainly hurtful. My temptation could be to take some solace in the belief that most people, when pressed as I was, would respond similarly. They too would feel as I felt, do what I did. Mine was a very human reaction. Sure, I cursed out my father-in-law, but only after he insulted me in front of my whole family. And anybody who says he would stay cool when attacked like that either doesn't know himself very well or is flat-out lying.

Such thinking would seem more rationale than reality. First of all, how can I really know how most others would act? My claim is a guess, one designed to make me feel better or to avoid scrutinizing my reaction after the fact.

Second, even if almost everybody would use as much volume or as many curse words as I, does that lessen the consequences of what I say? Will my wife say, "Whoa, you got really ugly in there, but you only did what everybody would"? Will the next family get-together have less tension, as the air was cleared (turned blue?) at the last one? When calm, will I be so sure about what others would have done in my shoes?

"Is it normal?" can imply "Is it abnormal?" Emotions can be judged as either too extreme (see chapter 2, "Problem or Disorder?") or too mild. If someone tells you, "I can't believe you're not more upset after what she said to you," what is she really saying? Is it "I know I'd be a lot more upset than you are," or, "Just about anybody I know would be more upset than you are"? Is she admiring you, or is she perplexed by you? Because you keep your composure and don't retaliate, are you being a little too emotionally self-stifling?

It's not uncommon for even-tempered individuals to be accused of stuffing their anger, of being emotionally constricted. Where is their outrage? They must be hiding it. They should be more distressed.

Isn't the measure of self-control the ability to show less fire than most others would in similar circumstances? Isn't it to act with self-restraint when others wouldn't and may not understand why you would? To quote the poet Rudyard Kipling, "If you can keep your head when all about you are losing theirs...you'll be a man, my son."[8]

In improving oneself, the goal is not to reach average; it is to move beyond it. As I tell parents, "The better the parent you are, the less company you'll have." The higher you reach—in love, discipline, supervision, involvement—the fewer you will meet at that altitude. You will move out of the majority.

Friends of mine have eighteen children, fifteen of whom are adopted with special needs. Is an eighteen-children family normal? Duh! Far fewer than 1 percent of households have ten children, much less eighteen. By the numbers alone, with or without special needs adopted children, this is quite an oddity among family structures.

An irony is that others' opinions of this family are not uniformly positive. One attitude is, "What are you trying to prove?" As Mom developed a near inhuman ability to navigate the roiling waters of her everyday family life, some admitted, "You make me feel inferior," especially if their one or two children were overwhelming them.

Anytime you conduct yourself exceptionally well, you risk being analyzed, critiqued even. Your behavior doesn't fit with the crowd's. It's therefore harder to explain. Emotional control is not an exception to this phenomenon. Good self-control will be misunderstood by some. Great self-control will be misunderstood by more.

The question "Is my anger normal?" is largely irrelevant. Whether it is or isn't normal, ask instead, "How is my anger affecting me and those around me?"

If your anger is within normal limits (says who?) but hurts you or others, it needs to be analyzed and challenged. If it's abnormal, in that it is absent when most think it should be present, be pleased: Yours is a good kind of abnormality.

TURNING THE PAGE...

Ask not, "Is it normal?" Ask, "Is it right?" The most typical reaction can cause real trouble. And the most atypical reaction can avoid real trouble.

Any reaction, normal or otherwise, is heavily influenced by whether one's expectations are high or low.

. . . .

Chapter Fourteen

HIGH or LOW?

. . . .

Want a good definition of frustration? Frustration is the difference between the way we want things to be and the way they are. It is the gap between our desires and reality. The bigger the gap, the more the frustration.

Parents tell me, "He's an angry child." With more details I often change the adjective: "I think he's a frustrated child when he doesn't get his way." His outbursts look angry, but at their core they are mostly frustration. Were Mom or Dad to give him whatever he wanted whenever he wanted it—in effect, to close the gap between his desires and life—his anger would vanish.

To reduce frustration we need to reduce the distance between what we expect—from others and from life—and what is. There are two ways this can be done: One, we can change others and life to better fit with our expectations. Or two, we can change ourselves. The latter is generally easier—or should I say, less hard—than the former.

Hypothetically, were I to drop my expectations of others to zero, any frustration in relating to them would also drop to zero.

After all, how can I be annoyed with someone for acting differently than I'd prefer if I have no preferences for how she should be acting?

Would this be a worthwhile goal? To harbor no expectations of anyone at any time? Even if we wanted to, that's not possible. No one can live without expectations. They're solidly wired into our nature. We expect to be treated well. Consciously or unconsciously, we operate by a variant of the Golden Rule: We want others to do unto us as we do unto them.

There is a crucial difference between expecting other people or life to satisfy me and having expectations as standards or moral goals. For example, if you are raising children, you have standards to guide you—respect, responsibility, morals. No doubt you are called to enforce your standards with discipline—lots. No doubt you also meet head on the reality that, no matter how clear your standards, your children will fall short of them—lots. So on one hand you expect right behavior from your kids. On the other, you'd best expect some wrong behavior, or you will be one frustrated parent.

Likewise, most people have personal standards. They know how they want to live or should live. It's a pathological individual who lives by few standards. At the least he shatters his own life. At the worst he preys upon others.

Our struggle comes when how we want others to live, especially toward us, doesn't match up with how they are living, especially toward us. One of the most common and vexing questions I hear is, in so many words, "How do I change another person?" be it a spouse, child, neighbor, boss, sister; be it another's thinking, attitude, behavior, feelings—in essence, some part of who the person is. How can I bring another more into line with what I believe is good for him or good for me?

Relationships, more so the better ones, are open to some influence. We can reason, guide, persuade another into rethinking his behavior toward us. Indeed, we expect that we should be able to. Expect it or not, we can't force it. We can't make another cooperate if he doesn't want to or if he sees little reason to.

And that makes our frustration rise fast and remain high. We can hope another will eventually see himself through our eyes. If he doesn't, however, our frustration sustains itself. Reality—a.k.a. this person—isn't moving.

A scenario: A twenty-year-old son has dropped out of school and lives at home pretty much on his own terms. He pays little or no rent, comes and goes whenever, is allergic to chores, and sits at the computer and its games for hours—interrupted periodically by working a part-time, low-wage job for gas and phone money. For over a year parents have talked, argued, lectured, threatened action, all to no net effect. Son's behavior hasn't budged. The gap between the way they want him to live and the way he is living isn't closing; it's getting wider.

In circumstances like these—becoming more common, by the way—I sometimes offer parents two basic options, both aimed at lowering their frustration but in very different ways. One, if you do not intend to take any definite action with your adult child, keep quiet. Cease the comments, nagging, pleading, disputes. Why exasperate yourself with these futile attempts to change reality? At the least your frustration won't spike every time your son acts irresponsibly or argues with you to just leave him alone.

Two, take action—from no longer washing his clothes or paying his car insurance to charging him rent or setting a date for him to be truly independent. Your actions do your talking. You change the present reality to better align with your expectations, and in so doing, you lower the frustration that's been hounding you for the past year. Sometimes you can change reality; more often, you can change yourself.

Is frustration distinct from anger? Not all that much. They overlap on the emotional continuum. And in its expression, frustration is a close cousin to anger.

Let's suppose you have a coworker you find self-absorbed and critical—in a word, difficult. And let's suppose you've worked together for nine years. And let's suppose you've outdone yourself trying to be pleasant and cooperative. One last suppose: He is irritating you more by the month, and your irritation is spilling over to your family.

What can you do? Tell your boss? What exactly would you say? "He's got a really difficult personality. Tell him to quit it." Who's to say your boss would or could do much to soften this person, particularly if he otherwise does his job? What if your unpleasant coworker is your boss?

How about confronting your colleague directly? Good luck. If one feature of his obnoxious personality is little awareness of his obnoxious personality, your correction, however tactfully worded, will almost certainly meet defensiveness or outright retaliation.

A social law: The broader the critique, the more likely it is to be ignored or rejected. Telling me, "You're thoughtless," threatens my self-view more than telling me, "You hurt my feelings when you said..." The latter speaks of a specific incident; the former of a personality flaw.

Suppose you approach your coworker with something like "You can be very critical," or "You talk a fair amount about yourself." (To my fellow counselors, pardon the "You" messages.) I doubt you'll receive, "Gosh, I've never really seen myself that way, but I do need to be open to others' opinions of me. You've given me a much-needed boost toward valuable introspection."

Assuming that's not his attitude, do you have any other solutions? Reduce your contact? What if your work requires mutual cooperation? What if this person, for reasons baffling to you, regularly seeks you out? Again, what if she's your supervisor?

There is one more solution, and it may be your best: Adjust your expectations—downward.

Your frustration or anger is sustained by any number of beliefs: I don't deserve such treatment; I don't criticize him. He shouldn't act this way. While true, none solves your problem. Why? Because he does act that way.

And he has for nearly a decade. You know beyond question what he is like. The evidence is overwhelming. If you were to calculate his instances of disagreeable conduct over the last nine years, the number could reach two thousand or more. If that sounds inflated, realize it's an average of one per workday. At some total, you'd better expect him to act consistently like who he is, or you will act consistently to upset yourself. You will put your mood at his mercy. He acts bad; you get mad.

At about age four, I was playing in our basement with a toy that refused to open. Enraged, I flung it against the basement wall, meaning to smash it. (I didn't know then that I should lower my expectations of the toy.) My mother, doing laundry nearby, ordered me to pick up all the pieces. My retort? "You pick them up." (Maybe I'm the difficult coworker, and the roots go back fifty-plus years.)

To add impact to my command, I began to bang my head—not too hard—against the cinder block wall. (I wasn't only a difficult child; I was a dumb child.) Now my mother would have to take me seriously. And indeed, she did leave her washing and move toward me. Putty in my hands, I gloated. But rather than reaching for the toy, she reached for my head, offering, "Here, let me help you."

My mother, like so many of her generation, wasn't soaked in the new and enlightened psychologically correct ways to raise children. She mostly relied upon instincts, good sense, and belief in an unalterable fact: I am Mom; you are not.

She wasn't about to be bullied or frustrated by my head games. Neither was she shocked by my actions, as her expectations of me were in line with them. After all, I was all of four years. If I insisted on punctuating my demands, Mom would echo the statement I was making. She wouldn't try to alter my reality; she'd enter into it.

I realize now that Mom was bluffing. I didn't then, and I learned fast that head butting wasn't all it was cracked up to be.

Much life stress is akin to psychologically butting our heads against walls. When others don't meet our expectations, we really shouldn't trash them, as I did my toy, but we shouldn't keep banging our heads against them either. If they're not about to yield, our attitude can. It'll save a lot of headaches.

In one sense a routinely frustrating person is easy to adjust to. She's earned her reputation over time. Each piece of negativity is in line with what you've learned, or are learning, to expect from her. More disturbing is the pleasant loved one—spouse, close friend, parent—who unexpectedly treats you poorly. She is acting counter to your image of her.

The saying is, "You can only be betrayed by a friend." An adversary can't betray you; you know who he is. It is the one closest to you emotionally who has the power to stun you with hurt.

Even so, the law of "Realistic expectations equals less frustration" still applies. The sweetest of people can get sour, sometimes toward us. Accept the fact that, as likeable as someone usually is, given the right conditions, he can act counter to character. Indeed, can't we all?

A friend of mine claims he is "over-wifed"—meaning that his wife is much more giving than he is. By that definition I too am over-wifed. Still, I must allow Randi the liberty to act less like her good nature and more like mine. (See, I too can be giving.) To expect all-saint, all the time demeanor is not only unfair to my wife, it also tempts me to get peeved when she doesn't act as sweet as I've come to expect.

Is the message, "Don't expect much from most others?" Protect yourself with the attitude "Oh, well, people inevitably will disappoint."

That's extreme. Rather the message is, "You will ask for needless frustration and anger by insisting that others, situations, and toys measure up to your desires, hopes, or needs." Moving your expectations closer to what is and farther from what you want will lengthen your fuse. It will take more frustration to frustrate you.

TURNING THE PAGE...

Like it or not, life forces us to readjust our expectations. Regularly we must raise or lower them to meet reality, which sometimes won't budge, despite our best pushes. And one key element in accepting reality is knowing what is fair and what is life.

Chapter Fifteen

· · · · · · ·

FAIR or LIFE?

· · · · · · ·

Within a few short years after his early fumbling attempts to talk, a child will fling his first F word. And despite his parents' tireless efforts to expunge it from his vocabulary, its use only gains momentum until it peaks in adolescence. In fact, the typical teen lives by the F word—*fair.*

"No fair," "That's not fair," or the very personal, "You're not fair," mostly flung at parent types, reverberate throughout childhood and beyond. The word is highly versatile, covering all kinds of discipline, circumstances, and people.

Parents are not without a ready defense. Citing paragraph 103-B of Childrearing Manual 101, they retort, "Life's not fair." Which only further convinces a youngster that the grown-up concept of equity is irretrievably warped.

Because "Life's not fair" doesn't pacify a child and, indeed, can antagonize him, parents could try another tack: "You're right. Life is fair; I'm not." I mean, if you're going to get unfairly accused, you might as well have some fun with it.

Most moms and dads do try to be equitable. They don't parent with a thumb on the scale; they don't earn criticism for bias. Why then do they get so accosted? Two reasons.

One, kids don't see life through a parent's eyes. When they cry "foul," it emanates from their own self-defined sense of justice.

Two, vigilance for fairness enters our consciousness not long after we're conscious.

Try an experiment. Select any two children, preferably preschool and close in age. Offer them one donut. Tell child A he gets to divide the donut for sharing and that he can cut the two pieces any size he wishes. Tell child B he has to pick one of the pieces first. Out come the calipers, digital scale, and electron microscope—all to insure that neither gets so much as one icing sprinkle more than the other, with all colors divided perfectly too. The drive for all justice all the time starts early in life, and it stays late.

Where does this drive originate? Parents don't step into parent-hood teaching little ones to expect everything to be fair and balanced. How do kids get the idea that it should be? From whom?

The Christian writer C.S. Lewis maintained that one strong piece of evidence for God's existence is our inborn sense of justice, for us and for others. He argued that a sense so strong must have an object. It must point to the existence of perfect justice for all, somewhere, somehow. [9]

Long before Lewis, theologians saw this drive as part of a moral code placed deep within human beings by God. They asserted that we don't need someone to teach us about fairness. The concept is rooted in our nature.

If so, is it futile to try to redirect it? Would we be battling our very being?

In nearly every sphere, life doesn't mete out abilities or experiences evenly. Some children are born into loving, moral homes. Others pinball through childhood with no stable adults anywhere close by. Some people are smart enough to pursue almost any career or vocation. Others' intellects limit their choices. All abilities, talents, gifts, indeed the very length of life are distributed unevenly across the population.

In the domain of personality, we all are loaded with temperamental inclinations—toward shyness, talkativeness, introversion, temper. They define who we are—up to a point. The rest of who we are can mitigate or exaggerate our inclinations, even the stronger ones.

Some kids are wired more impulsive than the norm, making their growing up a bit bumpier. Do we forgo disciplining them because self-control comes harder for them? The case could be made that they need more consistent discipline.

Should the garrulous individual allow herself to dominate every conversation simply because she's so inclined? Our desire for fairness may be innate, but that doesn't mean it lies beyond reshaping or that it has to be obliged in every circumstance.

Few people will quarrel with this. They may not at all like life's inequities, especially if they see themselves on the short end, but they recognize the reality, with their heads anyway. Further, most don't hold life responsible for its inequities. They don't view life as deliberately arbitrary.

Introduce other people into life, however, and intent is introduced. It's one thing for unthinking life to mistreat me; it's quite another for a thinking person to do so. She can at least try to be fair in her dealings with me. She has the potential, so she should use it.

Yes, that is true. But it does not mean she will. If she is able to choose, she is able to choose poorly. And regularly there is absolutely little or nothing we can do about it. And that sense of helplessness is what fuels the frustration.

While life may offer no guarantee of fairness, family life, in most people's eyes, should. Forging close emotional attachments, family should be the one place for fairness. Where strong emotions are involved, however, there can be exquisite equity or exquisite inequity.

A grandmother told me of her husband's stubborn unwillingness to treat his grandchildren with equal affection. To him the kids fell into two groups—the biological and the adopted. The biological grandchildren received his full share of warmth and acceptance. The adopted grandchildren were tolerated at best. Understandably, this bred ongoing tension for all family members, not just the kids.

What could Grandma and the parents do?

Reason with Grandpa? They'd done that to exhaustion. He wouldn't be moved. Further, he didn't see any need to move, for in his mind he had good reasons for his partiality.

Punish him by withdrawing their affection? That would pretty much squash any chance to persuade him.

Stay mad at him until he acts right? Again, that's not likely to soften his heart.

However trying of their patience, the family might just have to accept the fact that Grandpa is not going to be fair—for the foreseeable future anyway. And they will agitate themselves nonstop trying to get him to be. If anybody wins him over, it will likely be the kids.

Clinging to the expectation of fairness can push a person into counseling. Someone in a client's family or social circle has long treated her poorly, despite her repeated attempts to confront or correct the situation. Dwelling on the fluctuating injustice has become her mind's intrusive companion. Sometimes depression follows; sometimes resentment. Often the urge to retaliate is present, made more intense by the offender's seeming obliviousness to any wrongdoing.

What exactly is the problem with wanting life to be fair? Wouldn't people get along better if they'd treat one another justly? Relationships would be easier and more pleasant. Overall, life would be a smoother ride for everybody.

The problem is wanting something that doesn't always happen. You're left with two options. One, bring your expectations more into line with frustrating reality. Or two, get upset at uncooperative reality. (Where have we heard this before?)

When a parent tells a child, "Life is not fair," she is not concocting some false rationale just to massage his psyche. She knows it because she's lived it. Why then is it so much easier to instruct another about reality than to instruct ourselves?

The answer is straightforward. We flare when inequity directly touches us. It's another example of protection in service of the self. We are naturally inclined to worry more about ourselves than about others. True, that inclination can be overcome—think saints and parents—but for most of us much of the time, we are most attuned to fairness not coming our way.

Everyday life is jam-packed with inequities that can't be rectified: the job promotion one doesn't get, though he is clearly most qualified and all would agree, except the boss; the husband and wife who desperately want children but can't conceive; the adult child who singlehandedly cares for an aging parent while the siblings critique from the sidelines; the parent who poured her life into raising a child who now, for reasons unclear to her, has cut off all but the most superficial contact.

The list is endless. And each scenario potentially carries with it some mixture of pain and resentment. Living in the unfairness of it all, however, can cast one into a perpetual state of agitation.

In a perfect world with perfect people (Would you and I have to leave?), justice for all would be the norm. Until that day we'd better temper our demands for fairness. Like the preschooler who erupts because Mom gives more of the last cherry Popsicle to his better-behaved sister, we must accept the fact that sometimes we aren't going to get the cherry Popsicle from life. Actually, we might not get any Popsicle.

"Life is not fair"—words we've repeated countless times. When are they going to sink in? Alas, for both grown-ups and kids, sometimes the longest journey is the one from the head to the heart. Still, it's a journey well worth traveling, no matter how long it takes. At least that's what my parents told me.

TURNING THE PAGE...

Asking for fairness all the time is asking for frustration much of the time. Total fairness is an ideal, one not reached on this side of eternity.

The frustration at unfairness depends in part upon how much you *vent* and how much you *contain*.

Chapter Sixteen

· · · · · · ·

VENT or CONTAIN?

· · · · · · ·

It's a law of physics: To reduce the pressure in a vessel, provide an outlet. Give it some way to vent itself. As with the old-fashioned teakettle, when the water reaches its temperature limit, it seeks release.

Sigmund Freud long ago said something similar in regard to matters of the mind: Anger and its companion, aggression, need to be vented; otherwise they will reach a boiling point and wreak havoc on their vessel, the human psyche. Freud called this release catharsis.

Over time this theory gained a lot of steam and diffused into the popular psyche. And why not? It seemed so obvious, so basic, so, well, scientific. In one sense it is. Medicine is clear and emphatic: Lots of anger, particularly the ongoing, easily aroused kind, can do lots of damage—not only to one's relationships but to one's body. A host of reverberating ill effects can plague the person who doesn't find some means to settle his agitation.

All that is true. But is the reverse true? Pent-up anger is destructive; does it follow that releasing that anger is constructive? Asked another way, does venting anger—in word or deed—reduce anger?

For many, both inside and outside the psychological world, the answer is yes. "Once I get it all out, I'm fine." "I just had to get that off my chest." "Let it go, you'll feel better." Or the self-congratulatory "I tell it like it is." (At which I might ask, "Do you tell it like it is or like you think it is?")

Such statements reflect the prevailing belief that as one's internal state approaches critical mass, some sort of purging is necessary, indeed healthy. A parallel is often drawn to crying. "After a good cry I feel better." Sometimes a sense of catharsis does come with letting tears stream, and it isn't all emotional. Tears are loaded with the chemical stuff of stress. When they exit the body, so does some of the stress.

The parallel is not a perfect one. First, tears don't hurt anyone. Tears fall on one's own cheeks; angry words fall on another's ears.

Second, after the tears pass, the feelings accompanying them pass, at least somewhat. After the anger passes, other feelings typically follow—embarrassment, guilt, sheepishness, sorrow.

This is not to say that stifling swelling emotions is always good and voicing them is always bad. Obviously, the thoughts beneath the feelings ultimately need to be aired and shared. It is to say that discharging damaging words too readily can become an animal too unruly to restrain.

A chaplain in the military told me that, many more times than once, at peak upset he has headed into the cyber sphere to type his immediate complex of reactions to the offending party. He has learned the hard way to let that e-mail sit in his computer until the next morning. Very few leave his outbox. As he's concluded, "Send" is not your friend.

Few people feel genuinely relieved after emotionally erupting or verbally blistering someone. Most regret what they said or did. They later rethink what they initially thought was justified, wishing for a sort of reverse catharsis. That is, they'd like to be able to retract at least some of the fallout. Even if venting does have some cleansing effects, it risks exchanging one negative state for another.

Consider the course of a river. It appears to meander aimlessly; it does not. Water naturally follows the path of least resistance. It will flow where its flowing is freest. Observe too how, during a rainstorm, runoff rivulets of water seem to dig their own channels. Again, they slide down the path of least resistance. And as it rains harder, they slide faster and deeper down their entrenched channels. Future storms have a ready-made path for their drenchings.

Anger follows a similar course: The more it flows, the more easily it flows, and the more quickly it flows. It's dangerous that way. A vent can become a habit can become a style can become a personality. "This is just who I am when I'm pushed too far."

Still, stuffing all one's ire can't be good, can it? It will hemorrhage sometime somehow, often with little provocation. It will vent on its own. Even so, the critical question is, "Does venting—willful or not—have benefits? The plain answer is no.

Why do some insist they feel relieved after a vent? "I'm not as mad now as I was before I let it all out. I feel better." No doubt one may feel less agitated immediately after letting it all out. What exactly though is this feeling?

Emotions are in part physical sensations that our minds interpret. Consider grief, sadness, remorse, contrition. They are related, and which one at any time best captures our inner state is the label we use. Similarly, joy, peace, contentment, and happiness all more or less overlap on the emotional continuum. And which one someone is experiencing is subjective. What I call happiness you might call peace. What you call venting I could call erupting. What you call relief I could call exhaustion.

Suppose someone bursts into my office brandishing a gun and spewing a hostile diatribe. My immediate reaction is one of terror. In the language of physiology, my body is preparing me for fight or flight. Since the person is standing where flight is not possible, I am forced to sit helplessly.

Believe it or not, as time passes my fear lessens, if ever so slightly. While I remain absolutely aware of the danger, my body's inner storm is tapering. Why? Because the cascade of chemicals unleashed at first sight of this threat is subsiding.

Sometimes the body's settling is what makes anger decrease, not any type of catharsis. What feels like a release of tension could better be labeled emotional fatigue.

To pull it together, even if venting brings relief, it can come at a hefty price. A growing body of studies directly contradicts the old catharsis theories. Too much catharsis takes a toll, not only on others but on us.

Is it better to stifle your agitation, no matter what? Not always, as we shall see. There are better ways to express anger, obviously, or this book would end here.

TURNING THE PAGE...

Venting is good and necessary for dryers; it's not good for people, be they the venters or the ventees. Whether deliberately or not, we sometimes afford our anger too quick an outlet, with none too pleasant results.

To keep yourself from over-emoting, ask, "Should I be silent or sound off?"

Chapter Seventeen

. . . .

SILENT or SOUNDING OFF?[10]

. . . .

Recall the two sides of anger: the simmering—a low-level burning that can overheat unexpectedly due to seemingly minor provocation—and the eruptive—a more intense reaction driven by circumstances. The latter can be shocking, but it is more explainable than the former. And it doesn't necessarily bespeak some hidden emotional turmoil.

While simmering anger, especially when it boils, is more the stuff of psychological fascination, eruptive anger is more the stuff of everyday life. Most of us don't walk around in perpetual agitation, but most of us do have our feistier moments.

Further, these moments often seem to propel us to act against our better intentions. We really don't relish acting so badly. Few of us deliberately contemplate, "I think it's time to start riling myself up. I'll just need a few more minutes to reach full fury. Then I'll be ready to say what I wouldn't otherwise say."

No, like a scene on fast-forward, we find ourselves caught up in emotions, words, and conduct that can dominate our more reasonable self. While anger's rush seems reflexive, later we'll see that it's not as reflexive as it feels.

Most eruptions follow a pattern. They build rapidly, crest, and then—as the situation settles, as we settle, or through simple fatigue—they cool. It is during anger's crest that it provokes the most and the worst damage. If we were hooked to a sophisticated machine measuring the ebb and flow of our body systems, we'd see that our insides and outsides parallel each other in a predictable graph: Angrier leads to uglier.

Fortunately, even at our worst, most of us don't punch holes in walls, throw china, or fling bricks. Our display is not so much physical as it is verbal. It's expressed in words—insults, shouts, accusations, curses. Doesn't sound too pretty when all that stuff is listed in one place, does it?

Though it can feel irresistible, the impulse to lash out hard is surprisingly short-lived. The harshest thoughts make themselves heard during narrow emotional windows. Muting our words during those windows would dramatically reduce, even eliminate, the fallout to ourselves and others.

If I could rewrite my life, one of the first chapters I'd edit would include those occasions when I spoke from the rawness of emotion—sometimes not meaning it, sometimes half meaning it, sometimes meaning it only to verbally score. I'd put my family, friends, and colleagues into one big paragraph and write, "I take it back." For whatever I won by my words was short-lived, as I lost later in my regret and remorse or in another's reaction.

I suppose I could try to excuse myself with some version of "I didn't know what I was saying." But that wouldn't be totally true. Because I was emotional doesn't mean I wasn't in control—perhaps not fully but still plenty enough to be aware and responsible.

My professional experience confirms that were counselees more apt to restrain heated words, therapy would have fewer matters to resolve. It's universal: We all speak too quickly for our own and others' good. For the moment the heart beats the head, with unwanted repercussions.

A well-known shoe company has seen its sales skyrocket under the slogan "Just Do It." Apparently this injunction resonates with people. It speaks to motivating action through the power of the will. Would the counterpart, "Just Don't Do it," be equally appealing? Or more to the point, "Just Don't Say It"?

Cutting through the psychoanalysis, the repressed dynamics, and the search for the authentic self, much of good living boils down to a decision of the will. I will myself to act good and not bad, to speak well and not poorly. I decide.

Regrettable words and disturbing emotions follow a straight-line relationship. The closer in time the words are to the peak of emotion, the more likely they are to be nasty, hurtful, or retaliatory. If you can will yourself quiet for just a fraction of a minute, the urge to explode will lose steam. Granted, the emotional aftershocks can linger longer—hours, days even—but seldom at the same level of intensity. If and when you do speak, your words will be more measured, voicing your point more softly. Hard words, no matter how true, are hard for almost anyone to accept.

The sports world uses the phrase "addition by subtraction." It refers to a team's getting stronger by removing a weak player from the lineup. Lessen the impact of the bad, and you automatically improve the whole. It's new math: addition by subtraction.

Of course, to suggest, "Control yourself," at the instant of least control may sound akin to admonishing a fit-throwing four-year-old to just settle down. It might be what he should do, but he's not of a mind to do it, not until his mood passes anyway. Can we assume that the average grown-up has more self-control than the average preschooler? When was the last time you threw yourself on the floor or kicked over blocks? (You don't have to answer that.)

So the crux of the struggle is to keep one's mouth shut? That's a discipline far easier said than practiced. True, but most self-restraint doesn't demand sustained effort. The urge to sound off is at its peak for less than a minute. As the emotion subsides, so too does the urge to "speak my piece." (Now, there's a misnomer.) You won't have to work nearly as hard to leave unsaid what you know from experience you'll later wish you'd left unsaid.

The emotional parallels the physical. Longtime weight lifters not uncommonly can bench-press three hundred–plus pounds. Pushing against that amount of gravity is inconceivable to the beginning lifter. He must start at a number that is achievable but still takes effort. Over some years he may reach that vaunted three-hundred-pound plateau. What was once unthinkable becomes doable.

Holding your tongue (it weighs about four ounces) during maximum emotion might be comparable to benching your own weight on your first trip to the gym. But with measured repetition you can get there.

Make it your goal to conquer first those instances in which you tend to let your mouth loose but with some exertion could control it. Not every intense emotion challenges your self-control to the max; many if not most could be bridled with some exertion. Begin with the emotional weight you can manage, and you can work your way into pushing up some impressive poundage. But you have to want to do it.

For twenty seconds—OK, ten—say or do nothing. Stare (not glare), sigh (quietly), or look dumb (easier for some of us than others). Count the seconds if you have to. Find something to study—the ceiling, your shoes, your dog, the road. Divert your mind from your distress. Silence feels less and less foreign the more it replaces sounding off.

"I don't sound off. I speak my mind." Are you speaking your mind or your emotions? Speaking my mind implies speaking my thinking. This is how I see things, not just right now but consistently. "I wonder whether you even love the kids, given the way you berate them." Is this my durable impression, or is it a momentary accusation sparked by anger?

Strong emotions can distort our sense of reality. Suppose at the boiling point of a heated exchange with my wife, I blurt out, "Your parents raised a princess who still thinks everybody, including me, should be her subjects." How plausible is that? Will I still think this later, when I've settled?

When we speak our minds, we may be speaking as we think things are, not as they really are or anyone else thinks they are. I certainly don't want my wife to enlighten me about what's coursing through her brain at the very instant she's feeling most poorly inclined toward me. I'd prefer to have some of that impulse settle before she translates it into words.

Too much mind speaking doesn't do anybody much good. Indeed, some of the most hurtful, self-protective urges can roar into the head when one is feeling his wants and needs are being neglected or demeaned. Assertiveness can rapidly morph into nastiness as emotions drive the discourse harder.

"Sometimes I need to sound off hard to get my point across. I have to shock."

One of television's most popular early programs was a police drama. Routinely one of the lead detectives, after apprehending the bad guy and tiring of his excuses, would close the deal with a one-line verbal slap: "Maybe that's why they call it 'dope.'" Or, "Different stories, same ending." Whereupon the criminal would react with a look of shocked insight, indicating he had received some profound revelation about himself.[11]

Shaking someone with well-timed, well-worded comments, nasty or otherwise, is a staple of TV scriptwriters. Generations of shows, drama and comedy, have entertained us with the supposition that sometimes people just need to be hammered with an on-target observation about themselves, and self-scrutinizing change can commence.

The idea has merit. After all, we counselors aim for something similar, though without scriptwriters. Throughout the therapeutic dialogue we listen for the opening to offer a brilliant, life-altering perception that can uncover some hidden motive or pull together seemingly disparate threads of thought.

The critical difference between some of TV, most of therapy, and personal exchanges is one of style. Giving someone our version of the hard truth can be done hard or soft. In the middle of a clash, hard can take precedence as the points and counterpoints fly. In fact, the words can be well-aimed regarding substance; it's the delivery that invalidates them. A shock effect only works if there isn't too much shock.

Words can stun for many reasons. They are hurtful, they are accusatory, they are personal, they step on a live nerve, they are dead on target. I may intend to shake up my spouse's world, but my meaning, if spoken through a cloud of anger, can be lost.

The effect I think I'm creating may not be the one I am creating. Human nature resists accepting anything if it comes in an ugly package. The relationship is straightforward: the harder the words for another to hear, the softer the tone needed to get them across.

During a discipline disagreement with my wife, I might think I'm going to score the winning basket by shooting, "You're about as erratic a parent as I've seen." By tomorrow I realize what a bizarre exaggeration that is. By tomorrow my wife is still stinging, as much of her identity is tied to her motherhood, and my attack pierced straight to the core of who she is. If I didn't anticipate this, I'm going to experience it somehow, someway in the next few days or longer.

You just can't know how hard a sarcasm, retaliation, or verbal smack is unless you hit another with it and then watch the size and color of the bruise formed. That's very risky to both of you in yielding to a momentary urge to sound off.

Words that deserve repeating (without apology): You never have to say "I'm sorry" for something you didn't say. Recalling those high-riled moments when I stifled myself, I was relieved that my stupidity, hurtfulness, or irrationality stayed within my head. While I knew what was churning there, no one else did. Unless my wife can read my thoughts, which I wouldn't rule out.

TURNING THE PAGE...

Follow this rule: When you feel most driven to say something, don't say it. Even if you delay for seconds, the impulse to verbally blast will recede fast—if not every time then enough of the time to avoid heavy fallout in relationships.

Should the urge overpower your restraint, however, you have another choice: to be sorry or sour.

Chapter Eighteen

· · · · · · ·

SORRY or SOUR?[12]

· · · · · ·

"Say you're sorry." So have countless parents instructed countless kids over countless generations. It's one of Mom and Dad's earliest prescriptions for getting along better with others. It means, let the other person know you regret what you did and want to take a first step toward making it right.

Granted, as anyone with children knows, a kid's apology is routinely marked by an unspoken "sort of," or "not really," or "jerk!" My observations of my own children and others have convinced me that for the first several years of life, "I'm sorry" is aimed far more often at the floor than toward any offended human. If floors could speak, they'd probably say something like, "I wasn't the one you stepped on."

Nevertheless, long-standing parental wisdom has been that "Sorry" is a good thing to say, even if you don't want to say it. It's good even if it lacks conviction or flows from a superficial level of understanding. Parents know that the reality behind the words will come, if only inch-by-inch, over the course of a childhood.

Just as littler humans recoil viscerally from making apologies, so do we bigger humans. Children at least have a valid excuse. They are at the very beginning of their socialization. They don't yet grasp the value behind the words "I'm sorry." Their resistance is basic: "I don't want to say that, period. I can tell I don't like the sound of it."

We grown-ups don't like the sound of it either. No matter how much we might know it's warranted and deserved, saying those words means we need to leap an emotional hurdle. Like children, we resist viscerally.

Regularly I ask couples, "When was the last time either of you apologized to the other?" Answers vary: "On our first date." "Sometime before our twenty-five-year-old son was born." "Around the time Halley's Comet last went by."

You don't have to be a shrink to deduce that apologies are about as welcome a part of their relationship as a tax audit. More often than not, it wasn't always so. They did talk more nicely to each other once upon a time (and Halley's Comet does shoot by once every seventy-six years). Gradually, though, one or both spouses abandoned the practice and any desire to return to it. Thus the feelings wrapped around a good, honest "I'm sorry" died.

Silence is a giant first step toward self-control. "I'm sorry" is a giant first step toward damage control. After sufficient dust has settled, I need to make things right or at least make things less wrong. And few words begin reparations better than a genuine "I'm sorry." These two soft words can go a long way to counteract any number of hard words. One could call them the remedy for thoughts let loose in anger. Therefore, at the first or best opportunity, say, "I'm sorry."

That's it? Say, "I'm sorry"? You can say more, of course, depending upon what you're sorry about. But the revelation itself is about as simple as it gets. Unfortunately, *simple* doesn't mean easy.

The resistances to saying "I'm sorry" abound. To quote a psychologist friend, "Anything can be a justification for not doing something you really don't want to do."

"I didn't do anything wrong." Are you Mother Teresa or St. Francis? In nearly all ugly exchanges, it seems safe to say that, if you've not quite reached the apex of sainthood, you did at least a little wrong.

The old music group the Monkees admitted in one of their songs to being "a little bit wrong" and allowed the other person to be "a little bit right."[13] It is nice to acknowledge some blame. Most "I say/you say" arguments and put-down matches involve both parties, or they wouldn't rise to the level of nastiness that they do.

If I exploded, chances are really good that I said or did wrong, sometimes lots. Even if I believe I was provoked, even if I stayed cool for eighteen minutes before getting steamed, even if the other person acted worse, even if…

An apology is for what I did wrong, despite the fact that I'm convinced the whole episode was at most only 13 percent my fault. Whether 13 percent or 93 percent, I must be ready to take ownership (pardon the psychobabble) of my share. No excuses, no justification, no "So did you." Blaming some or all of my misconduct on another takes no self-scrutiny. And if I think my behavior is someone else's fault, I need offer no apology. On the contrary, I am owed one.

The point is not, "Do I have a reason for how I acted?" The point is, "Do I have anything at all to be sorry for?" You apologize for what you said or did, completely independent of how much you felt justified in saying or doing it. If you wait to apologize until you absolutely believe that the whole scenario was more than 50 percent your fault, well, when is Halley's Comet due again?

If I acted badly in anger, I—and no one else—made it happen. Any provocation may have felt nearly irresistible, but I did yield to it. No one forced me to react in the manner I did.

"I don't feel sorry." As my sisters would say to me during childhood arguments, "So?" Right conduct is not prompted by having the right feeling. If it were, much right conduct would go undone. An apology is a willing admission that some wrong occurred and needs to be addressed. If a "sorry" feeling accompanies the admission, so much the better. But it is not essential.

No question, in the fury of an altercation, the feelings that dominate will be anything but apologetic. On an emotional spectrum, a heartfelt apology and the so-called authentic emotions of the moment might occupy opposite poles. Consequently, to voice the most tentative "I'm sorry I used that word" might be a daunting task. What if your negative emotions are so overwhelming as to paralyze the slightest conciliatory impulse?

On to plan B: Apologize later, after the emotional surge has subsided. You can do delayed damage control. At the peak of hard and hurt feelings, you may not be able to bring yourself to acknowledge even 1 percent of personal fault in the face of the other person's 99. No way, no how, not now can you push out those wretched words of apology. OK, make it your intent to hold them in reserve until you're in a quieter emotional state. An "I'm sorry for…" retains healing power, whether it is expressed three seconds, three days, or three weeks after an offense.

And if you still don't feel sorry three weeks later, just try voicing the words *I'm sorry.* Good words without good feelings are better than no good words until backed by good feelings. Put more simply, saying is better than not saying.

"It won't be accepted; it will be rejected." That's always a possibility, especially if *sorry* is not part of your vocabulary. To another's ears any apology may sound foreign or forced, especially if she last received one during your wedding rehearsal dinner. If your vocabulary has never included the word *sorry,* you could come across as ill at ease and unsure of yourself. The words might seem as out of place to you as to her.

Nevertheless, rejection does not make the apology futile. If something is right to do, it is right to do no matter the outcome. Never judge the rightness of a behavior by whether it worked.

Sometimes an apology meets "If you were truly sorry, you'd stop acting that way," or "Sorry doesn't make everything right," or, "I wish I could believe you." All reveal a fundamental misunderstanding about human nature. One can truly regret his past behavior yet struggle to avoid like behavior in the future. My contrition over something I've said or done may be painfully real, but that contrition doesn't always guide me the next time my emotions misguide me.

With repetition, "I'm sorry" softens most recipients. The first fifteen attempts may bounce off resistant ears, but numbers 16 through 26, rather than sounding too glib to be genuine, can actually sound credible. They convey a maturity to acknowledge out loud—not once, not here and there, but however many times necessary—that I acted poorly. They speak of a more realistic perception of my responsibility.

It's a psychological paradox that words brimming with good for all involved can be a struggle to say out loud. Be the first to express regret, and doing so will get easier, not merely from practice but from receiving the reaction and reciprocation likely to come from the other.

There are no better words to begin the healing of anger's damage than a genuine "I'm sorry." They might meet a skeptical heart, but persistence makes their message hard to ignore: "I'm really trying to do better."

TURNING THE PAGE...

Being silent and being sorry work together. Practice silence during the fever pitch of emotion, and you won't have to practice sorry afterward.

However it might feel, even the most compelling anger is not solely an emotion. It is riddled with thoughts. To master that anger, the question must be asked: Is it based on emotion or thought?

Chapter Nineteen

. . . .

EMOTION or THOUGHT?

. . . .

Anger is pretty much all emotion. It is a feeling, a state of high tension. Or so it is thought.

But anger, like every other emotion, is more—much more. Anger flows from our thoughts—more specifically, from how we see others and the world around us. In short, anger has a major head component. To fully understand it, we have to look past the emotion to the kind of thinking that generates the emotion.

A scenario: You are attending a birthday party at your mother-in-law's home. You and she have always had a fragile relationship. From your engagement you've sensed that she felt her son could have done better in his mate selection. Meandering toward the kitchen to get something to drink, you overhear her talking to her daughter about you, and it's no litany of your attributes.

Remaining out of sight (Yes, it's sneaky, but the temptation overwhelms), you get an earful. And with each critique your inner temperature rises about three degrees. Fighting the impulse to storm in and vent some of that heat, you retreat to the family room in a mixture of shock and seething. You grab your husband and make abundantly clear that you wish to leave now, if not sooner. Your party mood is squashed, as is your mood for the next week.

In the driveway your husband ventures a perplexed "What happened in there?" Then he gets an earful, as you connect his mother to your distress. She was merciless, even for her. The cause of your pain is her rant.

Well, sort of. It is true, absent her rant—or at least absent your hearing it—you probably would have left later, emotionally intact. A more complete explanation, however, includes more than your mother-in-law. It includes what you are telling yourself about her and her kitchen commentary.

Some possibilities:

"She has no right to berate me—behind my back, no less."

"She ought to take a good look at herself—she's not the easiest person to get along with."

"After all I've done to reach out to her, this is my reward."

"What if my husband finds some way to excuse his mother and says I'm overreacting?"

Any one of these can ignite an inner burn, more so in combination. So let's scrutinize each.

"She has no right to berate me—behind my back, no less." At one level this is valid. The mother-in-law did indeed breach some elementary rules of family fair play. At another level, saying she shouldn't talk like this slams headlong into her pattern. Yes, she shouldn't; yes, she did.

Anyone, at any time, nearly anywhere, can act wrongly toward you, whether you deserve it or not. It's a social given that won't yield. Recognize and accept it, one small event at a time, and you will reduce others' power to push your emotions around. Disturbing you will take much longer. Maybe a nine-minute kitchen diatribe instead of a three.

"She ought to take a look at herself—she's not the easiest person to get along with." If she did look at herself, she probably would be easier to get along with. But are you waiting for something she seldom if ever does? And is your wait hooked to thin air? A rule of personality: Those most critical of others are least critical of themselves. I recall the wisdom about taking the beam out of one's own eye before removing the speck from another's (see Matthew 7:1–5).

"After all I've done to reach out to her, this is my reward." All your reaching out to her is your reward, independent of her reciprocation. That she doesn't act in kind does nothing to negate your kindness throughout the years. It just shows that she is not guided by the same degree of thoughtfulness that you are. Your mature conduct toward her is founded upon your character, even if she doesn't value it. If someone treats you as well as you treat her, count it a social plus.

"What if my husband finds some way to excuse his mother and says I'm overreacting?" Your mother-in-law doesn't think the world of you; you already knew that. Hearing it up close and personal only further confirms it. You would like to think, though, that your mate would understand you in this. And the possibility that he won't only magnifies your sense of isolation.

Possibilities are not certainties. You think your husband will fault you and pardon his mother. Do you know this for sure? Granted, he's done so at times in the past; nonetheless, this incident is unique in its harshness, unless you've previously caught your mother-in-law in the same act.

Seeing your high level of stress and his mother's low level of tolerance, your husband could be moved to your defense. While he may try to reduce the family fallout, he probably will align with you. Exactly how he will do both is yet to unfold. Don't add a "What if he can't or won't?" to all the other thoughts roiling your emotions.

To check any impulse to shoot off a set-her-straight e-mail twelve seconds after walking in your door, turn your attention toward you and away from her. Specifically ask yourself, "Which of my thoughts are most inciting my anger?" Separate your good thinking from your "stinking thinking," as one therapist has labeled it.

To be sure, it's nearly impossible to completely talk yourself down, even if the drive home is from another state. Your aim is to cool yourself enough that your steam doesn't linger in any future face-off with mom-in-law and that concocting a plan of retaliation isn't your following week's steady companion.

An emotion may feel automatic—a reflex response to an ugly situation or provocative person. Despite how it feels, the reaction itself isn't automatic. It's the thoughts beneath it that are automatic, often beyond our conscious awareness. Having been repeated so often and so long, they've become second nature. They are our immediate line of thinking across a range of circumstances, racing so fast that other, more deliberate thoughts can't catch up to them. They need to be slowed so they can be read and corrected.

We often speak as if anger just happens: "You made me mad."

"She really can irk me." "He frustrates me to no end." The sense is that another caused my emotion; I didn't. She acted, so I reacted.

Granted, she may have set the conditions for me to respond as I did. But a complete analysis of my emotion must always involve me. I'm an integral player.

It would be more accurate to say, "I made myself mad over her behavior." Or, "It irks me when he acts like that." Or, "I frustrate myself to no end when he's around." Almost no one naturally thinks like this, much less talks so. Rather our language underscores the pervasive notion that anger is in the main a mindless reaction. People and situations foster negative emotions, without my willful cooperation. In fact I need to look harder at how I'm involved.

Many counselors guide a process called cognitive behavior therapy. CBT has an older cousin, rational emotive therapy. The premise of both is that underlying our behavior and emotions are our thoughts. The goal is to help the client uncover the head stuff that is propelling his heart stuff. What exactly is he telling himself about some person, event, or life?

Next he is directed to rethink his thinking and to challenge his personal perceptions. Are they rational? Are they false assumptions? Do they misread motives? Do they anticipate a future not likely to ever happen? Do they give another's opinion too much credibility?

Let's return to the party—a safe move, as mother-in-law has since left with her daughter. Assume that she savored every tasteless word she uttered. Rather than swallowing her words whole, how can you digest them more accurately? Is she critical toward anyone who disagrees with her on anything? At the next birthday party, could another family member be her target, her daughter even? Does she demean others to regale herself?

Your answers are not excuses designed to invalidate any critical word you ever hear. They are meant to provide a better look at what is really occurring. And a better look can foster a better mood.

How quickly can a change in interpretation change an emotion? Picture you and me in the midst of an escalating argument. Abruptly I slap your cheek. How soon would you react? Right after my hand leaves your cheek, I'd guess. Your first thought? What is he—crazy? What's with him? I ought to slap him back—harder.

At one-second post-slap, were I to ask, "Why are you so peeved?" your answer likely would be, "Because you hit me, you jerk" (or some more colorful phrase). Immediately I offer, "I'm sorry," and point to a hideous spider scurrying away. "That jumped from your collar to your face."

Would you counter, "I don't care where it jumped. You slapped me, and I'm getting madder the more I think about it"? Or would you say, "Oh, wow, thank you"?

The fact is: I did smack you. Once your perception is reversed, however, from "You attacked me" to "You protected me," the slap lost its impact. You didn't have to choke back some version of "You sure are lucky, buddy, that there was a spider on my face right when you hit me." Not only did your sense of assault die at once; it was simultaneously replaced with gratitude or relief. When you made the slap the cause of your anger, you really meant the meaning that you gave to the slap.

Want another illustration of the powerful thought-emotion link?

Picture yourself jammed inside a crowded bus shelter. Gusting wind is blowing cold rain on everyone, as all struggle to huddle as far back in the shelter as bodies permit. While being jostled, you feel what seems to be the point of an umbrella jabbing the back of your heel. It continues, and your agitation begins. At that moment, if I were to ask you why you're upset, you'd probably answer with something like, "Somebody back there either is playing his idea of a game or is just flat-out oblivious to others."

Finally you lurch around to confront the umbrella stabber, to find an elderly blind woman trying to use her cane to stay oriented in the mass of shifting people. What happens to your anger? It's gone—right now, likely replaced by some other feeling, like sheepishness or even guilt.

What you thought was the source of your being upset—a jab in the foot—was not. The source lay deeper, in your perception of who was doing what to you. The instant your perception changed, so did your feeling. For most of us much of the time, rethinking occurs with new information.

Suppose you have just contacted the police in fear someone is lurking outside your home. Arriving, they knock, and slowly, with a distressed look, you crack your door open. His revolver unholstered, one officer commands in an intimidating voice, "Step outside please. Now!" With puzzlement and a little irritation, you obey, thinking, "Wait a minute. I'm not the bad guy here. Why are you bossing me around?"

After a serious search of your house and yard, the officer explains, "Ma'am, it's standard procedure to order you out of the house in these circumstances. We don't know who or what might be on the other side of that door or if you are being held against your will. Our aim is to insure your safety first."

How fast does your irritation depart? Once more, it's not the treatment itself that miffs you; it's your misunderstanding of it.

Can anger ever be a mindless reflex? Of course. Next time you stub your toe at 3 AM on your way to the bathroom, study your reaction. Probably not much flashes through your mind at the instant of toe-to-wood impact except pain. Within a few seconds some super-charged thinking could intrude. "I told him five times to move that dresser further back. He's toast tomorrow." And that thought alone could make your toe hurt worse.

TURNING THE PAGE...

Almost never does anger stand alone. It is driven by thoughts. And depending upon what those thoughts are, anger can remain under our control or can control us. Recognizing, refuting, and replacing erroneous thoughts are processes—in therapy and in life.

It is thus critical to ask ourselves if we are thinking rightly about someone or something. In other words, should we take an offense personally or otherwise?

Chapter Twenty

. . . .

PERSONAL or OTHERWISE?

. . . .

Not all misperceptions are created equal. Some are much more solidly wired into the human psyche. Thus they more quickly arouse ire.

Topping the list of ire-producing misperceptions is what psychologists call personalizing. As I mentioned in chapter 6, this means analyzing what another says or does and giving it a meaning that reflects upon one's self. In other words, "I'm interpreting this as a comment or attack on me."

A scenario: In the morning I enter my office suite. Two colleagues are conversing animatedly with each other. Nodding, I receive a smiling "Hello" from one and a hard-to-read, silent stare from the other. My first thought—a personalizing one—might be "What am I? Not deserving of courtesy?"

Walking toward my office, my mind starts its own walk. What could explain this apparent snub? Maybe she didn't hear me; she looked engrossed in her conversation; she faced a family crisis last night, and her brain is still reeling; the Muzak piped into the building was playing obnoxiously loud.

All of these in short order I consider and eliminate. I looked directly at her; she looked back. My greeting was within ten feet of her ears. She was laughing about something with her friend and didn't look at all distressed. The Muzak was crooning, "Put a Little Love in Your Heart." My ranking interpretation is that her stony stare was deliberate. She was saying or, in this case, not saying something about me.

That conclusion spurs on more *whys*. Did I unknowingly do something to rankle her? How and when? Do I have opinions at odds with hers? Have I said something she took wrongly, maybe personally? If I can't honestly think of my offense, could it be there was no offense? Could the explanation for this little social slight lie with her, not me?

I really don't know the answers, yet my first instinct is to take her face personally. For my morning's peace I'd better question my instinct. Someone's conduct toward me, however she intends it, is not automatically a statement about me, whether I think so or not. And I would do well to entertain other explanations.

Parents routinely accompany their discipline with "I love you, but I don't like what you did." They're reassuring their child: "This discipline is to teach you; it is not because I reject you or want you to feel bad." Instinctively parents understand that the pull to personalize begins young and has to be countered.

Often I meet with older parents tormented over their adult child's irresponsibility or immorality. They helplessly watch as their nineteen-, or twenty-four-, or thirty-four-year-old jettisons— for the foreseeable future anyway—the values of his childhood and family. And as his poor choices mount, so does their self-blame.

"Where did we go wrong?" "What did we miss?" "Why didn't

we see this coming?" The fault is self-directed, but it is misdirected. It is aimed at the wrong people.

Many of these mothers and fathers are conscientious parents who loved and disciplined well. And while parenting is a potent shaper of a child's character, it is not the sole one. His inborn personality, peer influences, toxic entertainment and media—to name only a handful of factors—blend to direct how a youngster matures or immatures.

Parents locked into an "our fault" mindset tie their emotions to their child's behavior. He acts bad; they feel even worse. What's more, they second-guess themselves and are reluctant to act decisively for their child's sake. For example, they may prop up a freeloading, childish grown-up for fear that by withdrawing support, they'll push him further down a self-destructive path. Convinced that they created this messy picture, they couldn't live with themselves if the picture grew messier. Personalizing doesn't only affect emotions; it hampers wise decision making.

Because the most intense of feelings live within marriage, it too can be fertile ground for personalizing. Wife is feeling belittled over husband's repeated failure to inform her when he'll be late getting home. With each no-call she becomes more convinced that he could care less, not only about her schedule but about her.

Hubby pleads guilty to the offense but denies its meaning. He insists it's not a sign of love lost; it's his own weakness, one he's been struggling to remedy with mixed success. If wife trusts his explanation, while still feeling inconvenienced, she won't feel demeaned. She won't wrestle with the sentiment that he doesn't consider her wishes worth considering. In so doing her being upset won't go so deep.

Personalizing can arise as much from overinterpretation as from misinterpretation. My son Peter is sixteen years old and lives to finagle for more social freedom. But I repeat myself. After some bout of nonstop negotiating, Peter manages to move his mother's mind toward his. Being a husband with more opinions than judgment, I observe, "He really can maneuver to get what he wants." Surely a benign fatherly insight about our son. But my wife, Randi, doesn't hear me describing Peter. She hears me implying, "You're not a very strong disciplinarian."

Peter's winning an occasional mom-son debate is no big parenting deal. Randi's feeling accused of parental weakness or incompetence can be. While my husband side may have been obtuse, my psychologist side should have anticipated that some remarks are just begging to be overinterpreted. Unless, that is, I'm not the most savvy shrink, and we'll analyze that shortly.

For thirty-plus years I have coached men's softball teams. Talk about managing teenagers! Who starts, who sits, who plays where, who bats in what order—all are my judgments, guided by multiple factors: ability, commitment, speed, age, injury. No surprise, some players have disputed my coaching moves. Their disgruntlement follows a pretty predictable base path: The more they read my lineup as a critique of their ball-player-hood, the worse they react. They don't see the many considerations involved in a coaching decision; they see one: He's putting me down as a player. Some feel strongly enough to quit in protest. Personalizing doesn't just make them mad; it sabotages their ambition—to play ball.

For thirty-plus years I have also been a therapist. (Yes, I only dared venture into coaching after getting a degree in psychology.)

Every so often a client will leave my office incensed over something I've said. Did I hold the therapeutic magnifying glass too close too early? I don't think so. I've grown cautious about making a premature observation that might rattle someone's self-view. Did I stumble upon some "accusation" he'd heard elsewhere? Not most of the time. Did I walk toward an issue that rested on thin emotional ice? Bingo!

No matter how soft my steps, my client heard me assailing his ego. Though I was implying nothing about his personhood, that is what he inferred. And he walked out in protest.

If I'm not careful, I could personalize my client's personalizing. What does his irate exit say about me? If I were more skilled, would he have stayed?

Suppose I did bungle a session, does that mean I'm a session bungler or, worse, a bungling counselor? To conclude so, I'd better have some evidence over time, not isolated episodes that may have other explanations. Resisting personalization is not making excuses for one's conduct; it is seeking an accurate appraisal of one's conduct.

Let's step out of the office into everyday life. Likely you've been staggered by someone's intense recoil to something you've said. Your comment was benign; you intended no offense. "Where did that reaction come from? I guess I stepped on a nerve."

Without meaning to, you touched a hypersensitive personal area, prompting the person to put far more weight to your words than you did. He personalized, and you felt it up close.

There's a saying: "If you want to make me mad, tell a lie about me. If you want to make me really mad, tell the truth about me." Only the truth can step on a nerve. Somewhere within I fear that your observation landed too close, and I resist it.

To generalize from an accurate observation to a broad personal statement is a logical error. This can't be overemphasized: A flaw in a personality doesn't mean a flawed person.

So how does one curb the bent to personalize? Several steps will aid you.

Step one: Look outside yourself. More directly, look toward the other person. What is motivating him? Is he hurting emotionally? Is he jealous of you? Threatened by you? Competitive with you? Does he like to argue—with anybody? Does he fling around his opinions as cosmological truth?

It's Life Principle 101: The most critical people are among the most insecure. Their demeaning of others' viewpoints is stirred by self-doubts or by a need to stand taller by stepping on others. When they criticize it may sound personal, but it's more their personality.

Among the psychological self-defenses is a granddaddy called projection. This is the tendency to ascribe to another the same behavior and motives one struggles with. For example, a husband with no evidence whatsoever relentlessly accuses his wife of having a wandering eye. Is he insecure, or is he the one with the wandering eye? His own inclination makes him suspicious of his wife.

Someone who projects will accuse you of faults and failings that he is blind to, or near-sighted about, in himself. And the blatant double vision can be real frustrating. If you're a projector's screen, know this: His words may be aimed at you, but they tell more about him. This is assuming, of course, that his criticisms aren't in some measure true. I mean, just because he possesses certain flaws doesn't mean you don't!

What if someone does intend to disparage who you are? He means to insult you as a person. No nuance accompanies his message, no separating your behavior from you. Even so, one question matters most: How much truth lies in his words? What wheat is there to separate from his chaff? If someone thinks me a total jerk, he may feel compelled to tell me. Am I really a total jerk? Or do I sometimes do jerky things? A big difference. Because someone wants to get down and personal doesn't mean I have to oblige him.

Step two: Critique the criticism. Much criticism comes not because you are acting wrongly or hurtfully. It comes because you are acting in a way the criticizer disagrees with. Your mother is adamantly against your home schooling, and she feels duty-bound to set you straight regularly. If she hands you one more article arguing against being a teaching mother, you're looking into getting an unlisted address.

Her stance is unshakeable; it is also irrelevant. As parent, you must ultimately decide what is best for your family, mom's criticism notwithstanding.

Your cousin is incensed by how you vote politically. He refuses to acknowledge your right to vote your values and conscience. He equates his views with the correct way to see the world. And because you don't see it through his eyes, you are stupid—case closed.

How can you lessen his power to push you? You could agree to avoid certain touchy topics, assuming he will oblige. If he insists on assaulting your views, distinguish helpful correction from personal opinion. It takes practice, but as you get better at it, you'll respond better to any criticism, fair or not. Always remember, as someone gets more personal, he gets less credible.

Step three: Stick to specifics. Back to the softball diamond. As an athlete, I am some years past my prime. My teammates say, "Ray was quite the player in his day. It's just that his day was March 3, 1983."

In my best years I had bad games in which I would go hitless or drop a routine fly ball. In recent years my ratio of bad to good outings is creeping up, as my body increasingly ignores my brain. Dumb body.

Why do I continue to play? For one thing, seven of my ten kids still live at home. A softball field is quieter and smells better.

For another, if I believed that a bad game meant I was a bad player, I would have quit years, maybe decades ago. Sandwiched between my poor outings, though, have been good ones. Such is the nature of the sport. As long as I stick to specifics, "I played badly," and don't generalize, "I'm a bad player," I can still enjoy the games, at least until my body forces reality upon me. No denying, at some point bad games will merge into bad player.

In counseling, a parent will tell me she cursed at her teen and called him names—not his given birth ones. Ever since, she's been calling herself names for her loss of control. In some cases long-standing hurtful dynamics are present, and the cursing is one sign of them. In others the outburst arises merely from understandable frustration, made all the more understandable by living with a teen.

In the latter case my feedback is fairly straightforward: Hitting your limit, you cursed and called your son names. Because you did, you are neither a terrible parent, a terrible person, nor a name caller even. You are a parent who did something wrong, which you regret.

Rather than thinking, "I did what I did because I must be the kind of person who does that," a fairer self-assessment may be, "I did what I did because I did what I did." Sounds too simple coming from a shrink, doesn't it?

As an aside, something tells me that the teen might not feel as bad as the parent. The bad words offered him a good opportunity to seek recompense. "Mom, can I have the car tonight...and all next week?"

Step four: Speak less trait language. Traits are the currency we use to describe ourselves and others. We rely on them because they summarize. They distill a whole lot of information into one or two words. Trait language comes with a drawback, however. It speaks in generics and is thus prone to mischaracterization. It does not capture the whole of someone.

"He's an honest guy." What specifically does that mean? He shares all his innermost feelings with his wife? He gives his employer 100 percent effort each and every day? He refuses to fudge a deduction on his tax return? He counts all his strokes in golf? When, where, and how is he honest? Honesty, like all traits, is expressed according to the particulars of time, place, and circumstances.

Consider the so-called angry child, who by age eight has thrown 612 temper outbursts. A crazy number? If Gale started them at age two, she's averaged about two per week. Mounts up fast, doesn't it?

No parent keeps a six-year running tally and then observes, "There she goes again. That's number 612. Still, that's less than 1 percent of her time awake. So according to the numbers, I guess she should be called a cooperative child."

No, the trait conveys a different impression: She's an angry child.

"My spouse is negative." "My son is demanding." "My father is controlling." All may be accurate at some level, but all are not accurate at every level. Which can rankle you more—being accused of making an arrogant remark or being accused of being arrogant? Your spouse calling your behavior thoughtless or her calling you a thoughtless husband?

Trait language can sting, whether aimed by another toward you or by you toward another. It can be the currency of insult. Use it carefully.

TURNING THE PAGE...

Personalizing is a short and well-trod path to misinterpretation. It puts the wrong meaning to words or events, leading naturally to resentment or anger. It takes one explanation—"This is a comment on me"—and places it well above all the others, which may be far more accurate.

How much the wrong idea gains hold depends upon whether you rehearse or reverse.

Chapter Twenty-One

. . . .

REHEARSE or REVERSE?

. . . .

If you want to get really good at something, practice. If you want to get really bad at something, practice. Practice turns potential into performance, whether positive—as in mastering a keyboard, hitting a ball, or putting words to a page—or negative—as in insulting, cursing, or thinking oneself into a lather.

Another word for practice is *rehearsal*. Rehearsal lays down pathways, in muscle or mind, that form ingrained patterns. And as these patterns become more ingrained, less conscious effort is needed to sustain them.

In college I played the organ professionally. During jazz riffs my fingers often moved faster than I could think. That is, they jumped from note to note before I could anticipate where they were headed. It was as though they had a mind of their own. And it was a good habit.

In college I also worked with a crew of fellows whose prime adjectives had four letters. In high school I seldom cursed, but in my new environment a habit, born of hearing and sustained by exposure, trespassed into my vocabulary. In a few months I was using once alien words without thinking. And it was a bad habit.

Rehearsal does more than form habits, however. Actors know that a believable portrayal involves more than memorizing lines. It requires immersion into how a character thinks. How exactly would he say what he's scripted to say? What parts of his personality need to be communicated, verbally and nonverbally? Rehearsal means stepping beyond the written lines to a role's persona.

Behavior psychologists describe human conduct with an A-B-C model. A stands for *antecedent*, the event or situation that causes B, my *behavior*. C is the *consequence* or the results of my behavior.

For most psychologists the A-B-C model is too limited. It ignores a critical point between A and B: the meaning I give to A. I don't react with little thought; I interpret.

Going back a few chapters, let's return you to mother-in-law's birthday party right after overhearing her kitchen harangue. I know, that's the last place you want to revisit. But in all likelihood, you did revisit it mentally over and over. And therein lies the snare.

Mother-in-law's conduct (A) prompted your early exit (B), which resulted in an emotionally bumpy car ride home (C). The interpretations you gave to her conduct escalated, driving your bad mood well beyond the ride home. Call those interpretations Step B-minus. Call dwelling on B-minus the rehearsal of the offense.

Rehearsal is a universal tendency. Someone wrongs us, as we see it anyway. Sometimes we react then and there, as our feelings goad us into action. As often we stifle our first impulse, storing the offense in our heads for later replay. Like the accomplished actor who doesn't merely memorize lines, we immerse ourselves in the role, scrutinizing it from every angle.

We analyze. "How could she talk to me that way?" We dissect. "Just what exactly did she mean by 'selfish'?" We refute. "I'm selfish? Has she ever taken a good look at herself?" We weigh. "Maybe I'll call her tonight or send her an e-mail. Or maybe I'll just wait and see if she brings it up again."

The mental monologue can roll on for minutes, hours, even days. It makes the provocation real again and again. It embellishes it and adds details, some of which occurred, others of which are only speculations. "She didn't actually call me selfish, but it sure sounded like she wanted to." "What if she starts up again next time I see her?"

A synergy is formed. The emotion fuels the rehearsal. And the rehearsal fuels more emotion. A hefty portion of bad feelings toward another is not caused by the original misconduct but by ruminating about it.

Suppose my hyper-opinionated cousin once again provides his unsought commentary on my "flawed" parenthood, not just to me but to six other family members sitting around the table. His remarks set me stewing, and I have to restrain my tongue to keep from sharing hot stew. To avoid a scene, I swallow my thoughts until everyone has gone home.

As the last car leaves, my stew reheats itself. I don't just re-chew my cousin's most recent put-down; I also dredge up a slew of his past ones. My temperature rises to a place higher than it was a few seconds after his table rebuke.

Yes, he got me going, but I keep me going, and to my mind, justifiably so. I have a whole lot to process. Still, who suffers more by my inner cooking—I or my cousin? He has no idea what I'm doing to myself. Maybe my wife suffers most, as she's the one who has to endure my audible broodings.

Mathematics talks of two kinds of functions: the additive and the multiplicative. In the additive the parts are added one to another to create a total, for example, 4+4+4=12. In the multiplicative the parts multiply each other for a rapidly increasing effect, 4x4x4=64. In an additive function, another 4 would take you from 12 to 16. In a multiplicative one, another 4 would take you from 64 to 256.

Rehearsal is not additive; it is multiplicative. Each agitating thought leads to multiple others, which then can lead to multiple others. To borrow more math terms, the accumulation creates a hyperbolic emotional function. In English, it climbs fast.

A common rehearsal is the inner dialogue. As I mentally re-listen to what or how someone said something to me, my mind recycles how I could or should have rejoined. Then I consider how she would rebut my rejoinders, and I fashion more comebacks to her comebacks. And so on and so on. Not only do I write the script, but I play all the parts and direct the action. Like a flow chart loaded with "If this, then that," my running dialogue can add any number of new offenses.

Much rehearsal is semiconscious. At one level I am aware that a stream of verbal agitation is coursing through my head. If asked I'll admit, "I keep working myself up over what happened." At another level it all proceeds so smoothly that the full effect doesn't register. I don't completely realize what I'm doing to myself. My thinking can conjure up a reality different from the one I faced an hour, day, or month ago.

Some years back a surprisingly unpleasant incident occurred at my office. Heading to my car for the one-hour trip home, my analyzing self walked with me. It seemed to me that I wasn't treated properly, and I was itching to chase why. How should I respond? In short, I was venting to myself.

With each mile toward home, my thoughts raced faster, and soon I was rehearsing at 55 miles per hour. Like my fingers on a keyboard, it was as though my mind had a mind of its own.

How does one put the brakes on a high-speed rehearsal?

The comedian Bob Newhart has a routine in which he plays a psychiatrist with a technique guaranteed to eliminate symptoms in under two minutes. A patient arrives, questioning how he can so quickly get results. He reassures her that if she does exactly what he advises, she will experience immediate relief.

The patient begins her litany of long-lived maladies, and immediately Newhart semi-shouts, "Stop it!"

Stunned into silence, she regroups and proceeds, "Anyway, I find myself thinking more and more about..." Again Newhart orders, "Stop it!" Each successive piece of her overthinking meets the same verbal wall.

Newhart's comedy isn't far removed from the world of therapy. In graduate school I learned a technique called thought stopping. Primarily it is used to suppress obsessions, a disturbing reiteration of unwanted thoughts. The goal is to make someone aware of her obsessions early in their trajectory and to emphatically challenge them with a sharp, loud "Stop!" The command is spoken by the client, not the therapist. And it is to be repeated whenever she senses her unwanted thoughts gaining momentum.

To cancel a rehearsal, the first step is to become aware that you are rehearsing and then to "Stop it!" Sounds too basic, doesn't it? A little too Bob Newhart? In fact, much inner upheaval gains momentum simply because we don't decide to end it. Whether by distracting ourselves with life around us or by challenging our intrusive thoughts, we can end a rehearsal by refusing to give it any more material. And with less material will come less discomfiting emotion.

Around the twenty-five-mile mark toward home, my rising agitation finally alerted me to my full distress rehearsal. I know, twenty-five miles is a long trip to insight. In my defense, I was also listening to the radio.

During the second twenty-five miles, I moved from working myself up to talking myself down. I started to reverse the rehearsal, mulling over ways to reanalyze the troubling event. Rather than personalizing it and retreading all its implications, I acknowledged the possibility that nothing personal was intended. In fact, I had to confess that I couldn't be sure of the person's motive. What I had been doing was speculating with little evidence.

Further, the interchange was not the person's style, so that left wide open the chance that something else was weighing on him. Instead of compiling options for redress, I pondered how pushing the matter could make things worse. In effect, I was playing counselor to myself.

You may not be a counselor, but you still do counsel, and for free. A family member or friend confides in you about some disturbing incident—not involving you—that has hijacked her thinking. Hearing her out, you offer better ways to think or cope.

She may not follow your guidance, but that doesn't mean it's not good guidance.

We give others sound advice for reversing a rehearsal. Can we do that to ourselves? Can we follow our own advice? Granted, where we personally are affected, our recycling emotions can hamper our reason. Nonetheless, the thought is well worth repeating: A bad rehearsal keeps emotions charged; a good rehearsal eases them.

Rewrite your script. Replace bad lines with better ones. This will lead to better acting and a better ending. In real life some scripts just beg to be rewritten.

TURNING THE PAGE...

Stop, then reverse. Key words to rethink when the rehearsal of a wrong threatens to occupy you. It's problem enough to misinterpret an event once; it's far worse to misinterpret it repeatedly.

Reversing will make it easier to make the crucial move to forgive rather than feel bad.

Chapter Twenty-Two

· · · · · · ·

FORGIVE or FEEL BAD?

· · · · · · ·

Alexander Pope is credited with the adage "To err is human; to forgive, divine." Often I've thought, "What exactly does this mean?" "To err is human" seems clear enough. The most saintly among us are locked into a nature capable of wrongdoing. It's the "to forgive, divine" part that puzzles me.

Does it mean that only God can forgive? That wouldn't seem so, as God calls upon all people to forgive. Does forgiving make one more like God—that is, showing qualities of mercy and patience? That sounds closer. How about the idea that forgiveness, especially of a deep offense, is divine in that it stretches us beyond what is natural to our human condition?

I've encountered many individuals who come to forgive horrendous acts of pain or hurt, so I'm inclined toward this last interpretation. The strength and humility underlying such heroic mercy amazes me. One could assert that true forgiveness of great wrong is only possible with divine help.

However the adage is read, one truth is clear: To forgive is good. But good for whom? If the answer is, for both the offender and the offended, the next question is, "Who benefits more?" A compelling case can be made that it is the offended, the one who does the forgiving.

When I hold tight to my ill will—Who wouldn't if someone did *this* to him?—it punishes me. My offender may have no inkling or only the slightest idea of my inner hostility. Only I experience its full impact, and almost always it hurts me.

Someone once observed that clinging to anger toward another is like ingesting a little bit of poison every day and waiting for it to sicken the other person.[14] An unwillingness to forgive can provoke the very outcome one is desperate to avoid.

Marital infidelity is a common crisis leading to counseling. As expected, the betrayed spouse is buffeted by a welter of intense and painful emotions. On one hand, she has always maintained that if infidelity ever intruded, the marriage would be doomed, as trust would be irretrievably shattered. On the other hand, given the many years of shared life, children, an uncertain future, and her spouse's contrition, her course is no longer so clear. She finds herself hoping to somehow salvage, even heal, the relationship. As studies show, we don't always act as we thought we would, especially when pushed to the outer bounds of our emotions.

The violated spouse asks, "How do I begin to forgive?" There are accompanying struggles: "Why do I have to be the one to change? I didn't do anything wrong." "After what he did, he can't expect me to get past this in a month and then live as if nothing ever happened." "I may forgive, but I'll never forget."

As I stress to every wandering spouse, "You severely underestimated how much damage your conduct would bring and how much time and effort it would take to repair."

When I'm asked by the injured partner, "Why do I have to be the one to change?" (often meaning "forgive"), I reply, "Because you too want to hold the marriage together, and without your cooperation, that's not likely to happen."

If she resists any conciliatory movement, not only does she consign herself to ongoing unhappiness, but she cripples the marital healing she hopes for. The end result? The marriage drifts downward, marked by mistrust and coldness. The offended one settles into an indefinite emotional deadness. The other, figuring his offense will never be pardoned, withdraws also. The frayed connection stretches until it breaks.

Fortunately, many if not most marriages don't have to weather unfaithfulness. Still, almost all weather everyday dings and slights, which call for some measure of everyday forgiveness. Otherwise, left to fester, they can become a pile too smoldering for either spouse to overlook. Forgive the small stuff, or it will become big stuff.

Mastering anger and mustering forgiveness follow the same path: Conquer the lighter load first. Back to the exercise analogy, don't head for the ninety-pound dumbbells; get the weights you have a chance at pumping up and down.

Life is not as ordered as a weight room. Out of nowhere it can press upon us a weight seemingly far beyond our capacity to bear. As with hoisting heavy dumbbells, however, strength comes with repetition. The more you persevere with weight you can handle, the more weight you can handle.

So it is with forgiveness. Much of the time forgiveness is within the limits of our strength. It is an exercise we can perform—if not easily, with a little extra push. And most efforts toward any kind of fitness—physical or emotional—begin small and progress.

"But I don't feel any forgiveness; I would be fooling myself."
(Psychologically speaking, it isn't always bad to fool oneself.)
Forgiveness is not a feeling. Forgiveness is an act—more specifically, an act of the will. I decide to forgive. I push myself past the
feeling that commands, "Hold on to the injustice."

How do I forgive if the desire to forgive is weak or absent?
Typically the lack of desire follows the practice of rehearsing the
wrong—what happened, what to do in return, how to answer if
confronted again, whether to take this matter any further...

Get control of the inner monologue, and the resistance to forgive
weakens. Rehearsing and forgiveness are antagonists. Brooding
won't allow forgiveness the slightest room to grow.

What if the offender isn't sorry? What if he thinks he did nothing
wrong? What if he's totally unaware of what he did? It's safe to
say that, more often than not, we think another person needs our
forgiveness more than he thinks he does.

Certainly if someone sees his wrong and apologizes, forgiving
him is less the challenge. If he doesn't, indeed if he feels justified in
his conduct, what then?

If forgiveness is good, then whether or not another wants it is—
forgive me—irrelevant. To tie my forgiving to another's willingness to be forgiven is to surrender to her my emotional well-being.
I won't calm me until she calms me first. This only gives her power
to regulate my mood. That's really risky.

What if there's nothing to forgive? Suppose my wife calls her
mother, asking for help with the children on an evening when
she'll be out but I'll be home. Given my touchiness about being
a mediocre caregiver (They need to be fed too?), I confront my

wife for making me look inept to her mother. (Personalization, anyone?)

After reminding me that I'm the child needing the most supervision, she maintains that she only intended to give me free time to work on my book about anger. (Oh, like that's supposed to settle me down!) Not only did I misread her motive, but I also had nothing to forgive. No wrong was present, only my oversensitivity.

I wonder how many times I've thought myself magnanimous in silently forgiving someone when his offense existed only in my head. I'm glad I don't know the total.

Helping someone separate a provocation from his own over-vigilance to offense is a theme in counseling. It's tricky terrain that needs to be walked gently. Few people welcome the idea that a fault lies in their mind rather than in someone else's conduct. The revelation that one's resentment or ire is grounded firmly in psychological midair is unsettling. Forgiveness has no object, as there is no one or nothing to forgive.

Let's move on to the core question: How do I forgive? Or better asked: How do I begin to forgive?

Step one: Decide to forgive. To restate, forgiveness is a decision; it is not a feeling. True, as bad feelings subside, they make room for forgiveness. And good feelings do follow in the wake of real forgiveness. But forgiving feelings need not be present to pursue a forgiving attitude. The notion that forgiveness has to feel authentic is faulty. If that were so, much in the way of mercy would never get the slightest foothold.

Neither does forgiveness mean some kind of warm, fuzzy disposition toward the offender. Ultimately that may come, but in the early stages of forgiveness, a lack of warmth is common. To forgive, one must first believe it is good and right to do so, feelings or no feelings.

Step two: Resist retaliation. Medicine has a guiding axiom: First do no harm. What is meant to cure must not instead damage. "The operation was a success, but the patient died." So goes the wry comment on medicine's limitations. Likewise, healing a relationship is impossible if I aim to hurt that relationship.

Retaliation is not an even-tempered attempt to settle a matter. It is more an attempt to settle the score or, at least, to tie it, using the same sort of ammunition that instigated the contest.

Only in math do two negatives make a positive. Have you ever resolved to tell someone "exactly how I feel" (too often code language for "let him have it") and were rewarded with "Thank you for telling me this in harsh words that I needed to hear. I will certainly try to keep your input in mind"? To paraphrase an insightful comedian, when a conversation begins with "What did you mean by that?" it doesn't usually end with "Oh, now I know what you meant by that."

In marriage counseling spouses seldom display an equal desire to change. One is more motivated, sometimes far more so, to make the marriage better. Should that spouse agree to curtail his or her verbal hit for hit, or hurt for hurt, even for one month, the daily friction will ease noticeably. Forgiveness will come more naturally, if only because there is less to forgive.

Earlier advice: When you most feel like saying it, don't say it. Bridle the urge to lash out for as little as ten to twenty seconds, and the urge will lose much of its intensity. At those times when I didn't speak as angrily as I felt justified to speak, not so long after I was unspeakably relieved. Neither did I need to ask for forgiveness.

When everything in you is screaming, "Don't let him get away with that," ask yourself, "If I return fire for fire, who gains?" It is tough to nourish forgiveness when one is thinking retaliation.

Step three: Want the other's good. What exactly does this mean? Hope he wins the lottery? Hope she sells her home for the asking price? Hope her kids get a scholarship?

In this context, to want the other's good means to want his personal and moral good. That could mean that he comes to see his fault, that he gains better self-control, that he has genuine contrition for his conduct toward you. To want another's good is to want what will make him a better person.

Why should you want that? The person is rude, difficult, or just downright mean. He needs a full-length psychological mirror held up to him, so he can see what he's really like.

This is not to suggest that you hold the mirror. But if life does, might he not learn from the view? And isn't that what you want? It is to anyone's benefit to see himself more clearly.

In a sense my desire for another's good is a desire for my own good. The more decent he is, the more decent he is likely to be toward everyone, including me. To use psychobabble, it's a win-win.

Christians are called to pray for their persecutors (Luke 6:28). What do they pray for? For insight that leads to repentance. For movement toward God. And as someone moves closer to God, he is better inclined toward people.

Prayer is not only good for the prayee; it's good for the prayer. Pondering payback toward another is much harder if I'm praying for him, that is, desiring his good. The act of prayer pushes out its adversary, retribution.

Step four: Know it's slow. In the words of a well-known movie character, "A man's got to know his limitations."[15] It's an unwelcome truth: Personal improvement is agonizingly slow. It is a two-steps-forward, one-step-backward walk. The most compelling motivation to improve leads to change measured in inches, not feet.

Almost all parents come to realize, however slowly, that kids absorb discipline lessons not over a month or over a year but over a childhood. A common frustration is, "I've tried everything; nothing works."

Often it isn't the child who is so far out of line; it's the parent's expectation. She wants maturation to unfold more quickly and smoothly than is real. And her exasperation only rises with the child's sluggish learning pace.

We adults are on a similar pace. In fact, the only people who change more slowly than the little people are the big people. At least the kids have an excuse. They haven't been learning all that long. They've not had anywhere near as much time to grow up as we have. But as the old dog might say, "It's taking me longer to learn new tricks."

Forgiveness advances gradually, even when it's most needed. Accepting this will help you continue to forgive whenever you're tempted to quit the whole effort. To rephrase the adage from this chapter's beginning: To begin to forgive is human; to persevere in forgiving is divine.

TURNING THE PAGE...

The greater the wrong done to me, the harder to forgive. The more wrongs, the harder to forgive. Were forgiveness to come naturally, it wouldn't be called divine.

Still, forgiveness is a practice worth pursuing with all one's strength, as it may be the single most sustaining force in any relationship, as well as being indispensable to one's own emotional well-being.

. . . .

RESAY or RESTATE?

. . . .

Painting the Golden Gate Bridge in San Francisco is said to be such a prolonged project that by the time the workmen finish at the far end, it is time to begin painting at the near end again. Reading a book is similar. By the time the reader gets to the back pages, he needs his memory for earlier pages refreshed.

So let's repaint, however briefly, the whole picture one more time.

ANGER OR ISSUES?

Words matter. They can clarify or confuse, simplify or complicate. In the updated language of anger and its behavior byproducts, words haven't clarified so much as complicated.

I don't have a temper; I have anger management issues. I don't have poor self-control; I present with emotional dysregulation. My behavior isn't wrong; it's inappropriate to the situation.

The best language is that which is most easily understood. If it doesn't come with a loss of understanding, simpler language is better language.

FIGHTING MAD

Shakespeare said, "A rose by any other name would smell as sweet."[16] So too with anger. By any name it is still the same. Yet over-psychologizing anger can move its causes from the self to some affliction outside the self.

To describe anger, begin with a simple truth: It answers first and foremost to the will.

PROBLEM OR DISORDER?

The boundary separating an emotional struggle from an emotional disorder is a fuzzy one. Further, anger's *whys* and *whats* are not necessarily made clearer when a diagnosis is attached to them. Often the diagnosis is a summary of what's going on, not an explanation.

Then too, a normal problem may cause as much or more trouble for someone as an abnormal one. Whether or not counseling will help is not automatically linked to the presence of a disorder. Much more depends upon the person and his willingness to work at improvement.

The effects of anger, not so much its name, matter most. Who does the anger hurt? When and how does it show itself? How can it be better controlled?

Diagnosis or no diagnosis, the causes and cures of troublesome emotions remain the same.

COOL OR HOT?

Psychologists have a phrase: nature vs. nurture. The question is, How much of a personality characteristic is due to genetics, and how much to environment? No surprise, but almost always any exact proportion is hard to measure.

Anger is an uncertain mix of neurology and learning. All of us

140

have inborn wiring that affects, for better or worse, how we react to others and circumstances.

Two conclusions follow:

One, not every emotional outburst is a sign of personal weakness. Biology also makes its voice heard. Some people just have a harder time taming their inner grouch.

Two, whether one is wired cool or hot, genetics aren't destiny. We are not automatons pushed blindly by our inner makeup. Each of us has the resources to enhance the better parts of our biology and temper the worse parts.

Nature provides the tendencies. We direct those tendencies.

SIMMER OR BOIL?

Anger is two-faced. More accurately, it is many-faced, but two faces are most well-known: the simmering and the boiling.

Simmering anger is a low-profile burn. It is sustained by a festering brew of hurts, slights, and injustices—real or perceived. It is mostly felt within, and only when it boils over is it felt by others. Because of its masked, lurking nature, simmering anger has the more frightening reputation. Fortunately, most people don't walk around in a perpetually percolating stew.

Boiling anger is an emotion surge, spurred by a provocation—from somebody or something. Typically it doesn't reverberate indefinitely, but at its peak it can be pretty obnoxious.

Whichever face it wears, anger is heavily shaped by a misreading of others' behavior and motives. Correct the misperceptions, and the emotions cool. The faces relax.

TRAIT OR STATE?

Why is someone Dr. Jekyll during the day and Mr. Hyde at night, honey with one person and horseradish with another?

Though seen by most as a trait—that is, a consistent feature of who one is ("He's an angry person")—anger more often is a state. How and when it presents itself depends much upon circumstances.

This can explain why little Angelina is a heavenly child at school and a hellion at home. Or why Hubby is Mr. Nice at work and Mr. Mean at home. The nature of anger is to be more controlled in one setting, less in another; more guarded with one person, more free-flowing with another.

To best fix fluctuating emotions, one must pinpoint the who, what, when, and where of them.

CLOSE OR CLASH?

Anger is pretty particular about whom it targets. Only a small group of people feel the biggest part of our ire. Sadly, those people almost always live in our inner circle—spouses, children, parents.

Ideally those we love most should feel our sting least. Realistically the opposite is true. Call it the law of emotional proximity.

Why so? For one, physical closeness can test emotional closeness. Living side by side with someone can challenge the reaches of our tolerance and patience. For another, we expect family members to act better toward us, leaving us more open to frustration when they don't.

The closer and longer we live with others, the more we know and feel their rough edges—and they ours. Accepting who they are, especially in the everyday of life, eases friction. No doubt it can be hard to keep composure with someone who is in place to irritate us daily—hourly?

We also relax our self-control when we feel most comfortable to be ourselves. If being ourselves means letting our frustration loose too easily, however, we would do well to work harder at not being so much ourselves.

A simple social rule: Treat those closest with the same demeanor reserved for those less close.

RIGHT OR WRONG?

The psycho-trendy phrase is well worn: Feelings are neither right nor wrong; they're just feelings.

At first hearing, this sounds so right. Upon a closer listen it unravels.

Some feelings carry their own turmoil—think fear, sadness, and anger. Even when contained, with no outward expression, they still can hurt the one harboring them. They as well can subtly guide how one treats others. Does being fearful make one easier or harder to get along with?

What's more, angry feelings are so routinely linked to angry conduct that the two could be called a dynamic duo. Anger seldom lives alone. It shows itself in one wrong way or another.

Among all the emotions, anger has the most potential to shatter the "feelings just are" cliché.

ALLY OR ADVERSARY?

Despite its nasty reputation, anger is not entirely a bad guy. Granted, if allowed free rein, it can wreak havoc on anyone nearby. But reined in, it can guide toward the good. It can provide valuable resolve. It can propel one to do what he should. It can override other troubling emotions, like fear and anxiety.

The key to using anger for benefit and not detriment is to moderate it by the will. Allow just enough pressure to provide motivation and not enough to overwhelm self-control.

Anger can be an ally. It can focus one's determination to act right and well. When disciplined, it can be one's servant and not one's ruler.

PRIMARY OR SECONDARY?

Learning Theory 101 says, Reward a behavior and you get more of it; punish a behavior and you get less.

Anger is not without some measure of reward. And that's what can make it inviting to misuse. Anger can manipulate, intimidate, threaten, or shut down criticism. Any of these can be a social payoff. Over time, however, the rewards will fade and be replaced by drawbacks.

Misusing anger is like taking a bad drug. In the short term it can provide a rush. In the long term more is needed to get less rush. And ultimately, even the heaviest doses will do nothing but hurt the host and his target.

Anger is not a good social tool. Use it to win, and you lose.

MY FAULT OR YOURS?

Self-control, self-restraint, self-composure—all have one word in common: *self.* Any kind of self-improvement must begin with the self. Until I accept the fact that managing my troublesome emotions begins within, it won't really begin.

No one and nothing can force me to react badly. Of course, people and circumstances can be provocative, sometimes exceedingly so. But the ultimate cause for my behavior points back toward me. As long as I look outside myself to place blame, I will be emotionally blinded. Inside is where my search starts.

The bad news: I may not be able to change others or life. The good news: I can change me, whether I think my anger is my fault or not.

MASTER OR MASTERED?

Emotions can trick us. Really intense emotions can really trick us. They can deceive us into believing that we answer to them, not they to us.

Despite what it feels like, anger and its buddies—frustration, agitation, irritation—are not forces that commandeer our psyche. We possess them; they don't possess us.

This is not to say that extreme emotions don't require extreme effort to moderate. Nonetheless, excepting some uncommon biological causes, anger must be seen as personally controllable. Otherwise it will only feel more irresistible with time and repetition.

To master anger, we must see ourselves, not the anger, as the master.

A RIGHT OR A CHOICE?

In an age of entitlement, not just the material is seen as one's due but also the emotional—particularly the right to be aggrieved. When someone wrongs or offends me, in my eyes anyway, I may see my anger as justified. It is to be expected, unquestioned even.

Discerning whether or not anger is my right, however, is a tricky exercise. How much anger is my right? How strongly expressed? At whom? When? Rights are not always black and white.

"Do I have the right?" is not the issue. Perhaps in some measure I do. The core issue is, "What will asserting my right do to me and others?"

We readily recognize an entitlement attitude in someone else. It's much to our benefit to turn that same insight toward ourselves. Anger is almost always a choice, not a right.

NORMAL OR RIGHT?

With much of life ever more scrutinized through a psychological lens, the question "Is it normal?" is supplanting "Is it right?" *Normal* is the new marker for a behavior's being considered OK.

So it is with anger. Its presence and expression are often judged appropriate by consensus. That is, would others in the same situation react as I do? If so, my reaction is inside the boundaries of emotional OK-ness.

The number of people who would do as I do is not a good gauge of the goodness of my conduct. Frustrating, hurtful, and mean behavior can have lots of players.

A healthy goal, morally and psychologically speaking, is not to be within the norm of self-control. It is to be above the norm—well above.

HIGH OR LOW?

Frustration has been defined as the difference between what we want and what is. The bigger the gap, the more the frustration.

To lower frustration we have two options: Bring reality more into line with our desires, or bring our desires more into line with reality. Given that reality can be real tough, if not impossible, to move, the best option is to move ourselves—more specifically, our expectations.

Lowering expectations is not some sort of social surrender. Nor does it mean tolerating lower standards. Rather it can be a healthy acceptance of what is. And what is, is that we will always face some people who will not change to suit us and a life that won't either.

Accepting this none too agreeable reality will bring a dramatic benefit: It will greatly reduce frustration.

FAIR OR LIFE?

Life is not fair. A cliché, oft repeated. All clichés have fragments of truth, or they wouldn't have gotten their start toward being clichés. This cliché is of a different kind. It is all truth. Indeed, life is not fair.

Everyone who has a life knows this. Not everyone believes it or, if he does believe it, likes it. Asking that life be fair is asking for lifelong upset.

Yes, how much better it would be if things were parceled out evenly or if others would always act with justice toward us. Not in this world will it happen, ever.

When what we want or demand evades us, hard feelings can follow. The more we can accept in our hearts what we know in our heads, the less our resistance to this most valid cliché.

VENT OR CONTAIN?

Conventional wisdom has long advised that anger vented is good. It allows stress a release, much like the pressure discharged from a steam valve. Conventional wisdom isn't always wise or always true.

This piece of conventional wisdom is now being rethought. It seems that venting anger, especially rashly, can cause the venter a number of ill effects.

One, anger too often expressed leads to it being expressed more often. Blowing off steam comes sooner and easier with less pressure.

Two, venting can take a physical toll on its releaser. It agitates rather than pacifies.

And three, loud and long anger can generate distress post-vent: guilt, shame, embarrassment, and regret.

A piece of wisdom: Moderating one's emotional expression is a healthier alternative to letting it flow.

SILENT OR SOUNDING OFF?

For almost everybody the unleashed tongue causes trouble. As emotions peak, the heat of accompanying words peaks too. Lock the tongue behind its walls of teeth during those moments, and the compulsion to speak one's rampaging mind dissipates. The words we feel most driven to fire off will lose enough heat to allow us to keep them inside, thus averting real spoken damage.

The connection is simple and straightforward: The hotter the emotions, the harsher our words. And the more we later wish we could unsay them.

Passive control is generally easier to exert than active control. Meaning, staying silent is easier—less hard?—than trying to replace bad words with good ones at the zenith of emotions. Let silence speak for a short while, and better words will come more easily afterward.

SORRY OR SOUR?

Even the best disciplined of tongues does damage on occasion. Few of us can navigate more than a few days—a few weeks at most—without emotion-driven words that hurt someone somehow. So when they do, follow with damage control or relationship restoration. Say, "I'm sorry."

If your apology is rejected, or if you don't feel sorry, or if you believe any fault is at most 6 percent yours, apologize anyway. Practice the words, and with repetition they will become more natural. So will the appreciation of the person receiving the apology.

Anger can feel spontaneous, but an apology is always deliberate. Few words can better neutralize the toxic effects of what came before than "I'm sorry."

You never have to apologize for what you don't say. But if you do say it, be ready to apologize, if not sooner, then later.

EMOTION OR THOUGHT?

Anger is thought to be pretty much all emotion. But in fact anger has a heavy head component. How we think drives how we feel.

Events don't automatically cause anger. Neither do people. It is our interpretation of those events and people that affects us. We give meaning to it all. And the meaning we give can calm us or rouse us to fury.

Much anger is fueled by irrational, self-defeating, or just plain wrong thinking. Seeing how and when such thinking is misleading us may well be the most potent strategy for settling turbulent emotions.

It's an inseparable relationship: Better thinking means better emotions.

PERSONAL OR OTHERWISE?

The instinct for self-preservation is wired deeply. We are powerfully moved to protect ourselves, not only physically but emotionally.

In the language of counseling, the word is *personalization*. It is the tendency to interpret another's actions as a comment, insult even, to one's personhood.

The problems with personalization are many, but two stand out. One, someone else's behavior may have little or nothing to do with me, even if he intends it so. It is personal, all right, but personal to him.

Two, personalizing leads to a hypervigilance that will predispose me to peevishness in my relationships.

Personalization arguably heads the list of misperceptions that foster overreaction. Look first for accurate explanations for another's behavior.

REHEARSE OR REVERSE?

Practice may make perfect, but some skills you don't want to perfect. They only make you good at doing what isn't good for you. When the misguided thinking underlying anger is embellished and dwelled upon, the anger is magnified.

Rehearsal makes anger linger, as the inner dialogue rehashes the particulars and implications of the original offense. With practice, rehearsals become habit, an automatic response to frustration.

The first step in cancelling a rehearsal is to become aware of its presence. Realize when something negative is cycling in the head. The second step is to rewrite the script. Replace the bad lines with good ones.

FORGIVE OR FEEL BAD?

Forgiveness is not foremost a feeling. It is foremost a decision, a conscious act of the will. And that's good, as over life's long haul, the will is a more stable guide than the emotions. If one waits for bad feelings to subside on their own or for good feelings to replace them, forgiveness, at a minimum, will be delayed, if not abandoned indefinitely.

Resentments and agitations reverberate much longer if we don't give forgiveness a chance. Forgiveness is not just good for the forgiven. It is as good, if not more so, for the forgiver.

No single act can relieve the corrosive aftereffects of anger more than an honest act of forgiveness. To be sure, forgiving is hard, especially when the offender isn't sorry. Only one thing is harder: not forgiving.

Notes

• • • • • • •

1. Ravi Zacharias, "Crux of the Story," A Slice of Infinity, Ravi Zacharias International Ministries, July 5, 2012, http://www.rzim.org/a-slice-of-infinity/crux-of-the-story/.
2. Steve Skrovan and Ray Romano, "Getting Even," *Everybody Loves Raymond*, season 3, episode 4, directed by Steve Zuckerman, aired October 12, 1998.
3. Danny DeVito as Sam Stone in *Ruthless People*, directed by Jim Abrahams, David Zucker, and Jerry Zucker (Touchstone Pictures, 1986).
4. Robert Burns, "To a Louse," verse 8.
5. Don Schlitz, "The Gambler."
6. Matraca Maria Berg, "You Can Feel Bad."
7. Fulton Sheen, *Old Errors and New Labels* (New York: Society of St. Paul/Alba House, 2007).
8. Rudyard Kipling, "If."
9. C.S. Lewis, *Mere Christianity* (New York: Macmillan, 1943), pp. 45–46.
10. Parts of this chapter are excerpted from my book *Marriage: Small Steps, Big Rewards* (Cincinnati: Servant, 2011).
11. Jack Webb, *Dragnet*, 1951–1959.
12. Parts of this chapter are excerpted from *Marriage: Small Steps, Big Rewards*.
13. The Monkees, "A Little Bit Me, a Little Bit You."
14. This is often credited to Buddha.
15. Clint Eastwood as policeman Harry Callahan in *Magnum Force*, directed by Ted Post (Warner Bros., 1973).
16. William Shakespeare, *Romeo and Juliet*, act 2, scene 2.

ABOUT THE AUTHOR

Dr. Ray Guarendi is a father of ten, clinical psychologist, author, public speaker, and nationally syndicated radio host. His radio show, *The Doctor Is In,* can be heard weekdays on Ave Maria Radio, EWTN, and Sirius XM. Dr. Ray also hosts his own TV show, *Living Right with Dr. Ray.* His books include *Discipline That Lasts a Lifetime; Good Discipline, Great Teens;* and *Winning the Discipline Debates.*